How to Write Parallel Programs

A First Course

How to Write Parallel Programs
A First Course

Nicholas Carriero
David Gelernter

The MIT Press
Cambridge, Massachusetts
London, England

This book was printed and bound in the United States of America.

Library of Congress Cataloging-in-Publication Data

Carriero, Nicholas.
     How to write parallel programs: a first course / Nicholas Carriero, David Gelernter.
          p.   cm.
     Includes bibliographical references and index.
     ISBN 0-262-03171-X
     1. Parallel programming (Computer science) I. Gelernter, David Hillel. II. Title.
     QA76.642.C37   1990   90-44443
     005.2--dc20   CIP

For D. and J.P. and in memory of
M.R.C. who, having taught, teaches still.

For my parents, the Sibs, Daniel
and Jane—

Ein Blick von dir, Ein Wort mehr unterhält
Als alle Weisheit dieser Welt.

Contents

Contents

List of Figures

List of Figures

Preface

This book is the raw material for a hands-on, "workshop" type course for undergraduates or graduate students in parallel programming. It can also serves as the core of a more conventional course; and it might profitably be read (we hope and believe) by any professional or researcher who needs an up-to-date synthesis of this fast-growing, fast-changing and fast-maturing field.

By a "workshop" course we mean a course in which student projects play a major part. The exercise sections at the end of each chapter are integral to the text; everyone who consults this book should (at least) read them. Problems in chapters 2 through 5 lay the groundwork; the exercise sections in the last four chapters each center on a detailed investigation of a real and substantial problem. For students who pursue them seriously, these programming problems will require time, care and creativity. In most cases they lack stereotyped solutions. Discussion of student efforts can and ought to play a significant part in class meetings.

The programming examples and exercises use C-Linda[1]; C-Linda running on a parallel machine or a network is the ideal lab environment for the workshop course we've described. A C-Linda simulator running on a standard workstation is an adequate environment. Relying on some other parallel language or programming system is perfectly okay as well. The called-for translations between the book and the lab environment might be slightly painful (particularly if the non-Linda parallel language you choose is any variant of the ubiquitous message-passing or remote-procedure-call models), but these translation exercises are always illuminating, and anyway, they build character.

The "more conventional" course we mentioned would deal with parallel systems in general. Parallel *software* is still the heart and soul of such a course, but teachers should add some material to what is covered in this book. We would arrange the syllabus for such a course as follows:

1. *Introduction and basic paradigms.* (The first two chapters of this text.)

2. *Machine architectures for parallelism.* We'd use chapter 21 of

---

[1]Linda is a registered trademark of Scientific Computing Associates.

Ward and Halstead's *Computation Structures* [WH90], or part 3 of Almasi and Gottlieb's *Highly Parallel Computing* [AG89].

3. *Linda, and parallel programming basics.* (Chapter 3.)

4. *Parallel languages and systems other than Linda; two special-purpose models of parallelism: data-parallelism and systolic systems.* The most comprehensive and up-to-date overview of parallel languages and systems is Bal, Steiner and Tanenbaum's survey paper on "Programming languages for distributed computing systems" [BST89]. (A brief survey appears in section 2.6 of this book.) Hillis and Steele's paper on "Data parallel algorithms" [HS86] is a good introduction to data parallelism; Kung and Leiserson's paper on "Systolic arrays (for VLSI)" [KL79] is the classic presentation of systolic programming.

   This section ought to make a point of asking (among other questions) how Linda differs from a horde of competitors. The Bal *et al.* paper discusses Linda in context, as does Ben-Ari's *Principles of Concurrent and Distributed Programming* [BA90] (which is mainly about Ada but has good discussions of occam and Linda as well), the parallel languages chapter of Gelernter and Jagannathan's *Programming Linguistics* [GJ90], and the authors' paper on "Linda in context" [CG89].

5. *Writing parallel programs:* the rest of the text.

Acknowledgments

Many people contributed enormously to the effort that culminated in this book. First, the Linda group at Yale: particularly (in order of appearance) Jerry Leichter, Rob Bjornson, Venki Krishnaswamy, Mike Factor and Susanne Hupfer; many thanks, too, to Paul Bercovitz, Scott Fertig, Jim Philbin and Stephen Zenith. The second author acknowledges with particular satisfaction the help, contributions and advice of two of the same people he mentioned in his thesis seven years ago: Mauricio Arango and Suresh Jagannathan. Both authors are grateful for the help and support of their colleagues and friends at Bell Labs, particularly Sid Ahuja and Tom London.

We will always be grateful to Dick Lau of the Office of Naval Research for funding support that made our work possible. The National Science Foundation has been a friend and indispensable supporter of our research in good times and bad, and a model of seriousness and integrity in all its dealings. Chris Hatchell, our administrative assistant and group manager-coordinator, set new standards. We are much indebted to him for years of brilliant, indispensable helpfulness. And we thank our international visitors, and the research groups around the world who have kept us informed about their work on and with Linda.

But in the end, our acknowledgments come down to one man. If the discipline of computer science had a man of the decade during the 1980's, our candidate would be Martin Schultz. For many of those years Martin was chairman of the department at Yale; for all them, he was a leader of the field. Martin saw clearly that *significant* contributions to computer systems research (*vs.* mere academic wheel-spinning) require hardware *and* systems research *and* real applications. When you put those ingredients together (he thought) the reaction might be spectacular; it might illuminate the field. He was right. He had a vision, he put it into effect, and wonderful things happened. Thanks, Martin—

Nicholas Carriero
David Gelernter

1 Introduction

This introduction addresses three topics: what we propose to do in this book, why we claim it's important and how we propose to do it.

1.1 What?

One way to solve a problem fast is to break the problem into pieces, and arrange for all the pieces to be solved simultaneously. The more pieces, the faster the job goes—up to a point where the pieces become too small to make the effort of breaking-up and distributing worth the bother. These simple, obvious observations underlie all of parallel programming. A "parallel program" is a program that uses the breaking-up and handing-out approach to solve large or difficult problems. This book's master plan is to transform "ordinary" programmers into parallel programmers.

Parallelism, we claimed, is one way to solve problems fast. Actually, it is *the* way. Throughout human problem-solving history, complex engineering and organizational problems have been attacked and mastered by using parallelism. Complex organizations are managed, large buildings built and formidable enemies defeated by bunches of workers, not by isolated actors. A watch, a steam engine or a factory is built up out of many simultaneously-active components.

Parallelism is the norm; purely *sequential* problem solving is the anomalous restriction. In the early history of computing, the anomaly developed for good reasons. Processors were expensive, and throwing many of them at one problem rarely made sense. More important, people mistook programming for the mere transcription of algorithms into machine-executable form. We understand now that building software machinery is an organizational and engineering challenge of the first order.

All of which is not to say that sequential programming is no longer important. It will remain the technique of choice for solving small problems; it is the indispensable basis for the parallel techniques we discuss in this book. It remains fundamental. When you learn how to paint, you don't forget how to draw. But no serious programmer will want to restrict his technical capabilities to black and white now that color has arrived.

Early in the "parallel computing age" (around ten years ago, let's say), software pundits used to claim that it would be hard to find programs that could be "parallelized". After all, most ordinary programs are conceived in terms of *sequences* of activities: "do step 1, then do step 2,..." How often would this kind of program prove to be transformable into a parallel code—"do the following n steps *at the same time?*" As things turned out, it's hard to find a large problem that *can't* benefit from parallelism. Not all algorithms benefit to the same extent, of course, but algorithms that don't parallelize can often be replaced by algorithms that work better. Parallelism sees active ("production") use today in numerical problem solving, simulation of large physical and engineering systems, graphics, database manipulation and other areas. Its potential significance in the near future is enormous. We'll pursue these points below.

Parallel programs are intended for execution on many processors simultaneously. Each processor works on one piece of the problem, and they all proceed together. In the best case, n processors focussed on a single problem will solve it n times faster than any single processor. We can't routinely achieve this "ideal linear speedup" in practice, but parallelism is a proven way to run a large variety of real and important programs fast.

The many processors on which a parallel program executes may all be packed into one box (yielding a "multiprocessor" or "parallel computer") or they may be separate, autonomous machines connected by a network. A multiprocessor might encompass a few processors or thousands; its processors might be inter-connected using any of a large number of schemes. The network might be local or wide-area; the computers in the network might be anything. Note, however, that this book isn't about parallel programming "for hypercube-connected multiprocessors" or "on Ethernet-connected local area nets" or "for the EnnuiTec SX (models 38 through 42)". It deals with parallel programming *in general*, using *any* kind of processor ensemble. Our only restriction is that we focus on "asynchronous parallelism"—parallelism in which (roughly speaking) each separate process or locus of activity can do whatever it wants. "Synchronous parallelism" is a specialized form in which all activities proceed in lock step, doing essentially the same thing at the same time. We discuss this specialized form only in passing.

The main focus, and two side-issues. We concentrate mainly on parallel programming for current-generation parallel machines and networks. Such environments usually encompass anywhere from several through several hundred processors. Inter-processor communication is fast in some of these settings (the shared-memory multiprocessors), but fairly slow in others and *very* slow in some. A slow-communication environment can be a challenging one for parallel program development, for reasons we will discuss (and which are probably obvious in any case). Nonetheless, many useful and powerful platforms for parallel computing *are* slow-communication environments. The program development techniques we present in this book aren't speculative; they are designed to take real conditions into account. Programmers who master them will be prepared for a wide variety of environments, including hostile ones.

The book has two subsidiary focusses as well. Neither is treated in depth, but we glance at both repeatedly.

One is *massive parallelism* (massive *asynchronous* parallelism specifically). Parallel machines encompassing ten thousand powerful processors or more are now in design. Building software for these machines will be a major technical challenge. In fact, merely figuring out what to *do* with them will be a challenge: what kind of applications will be capable of consuming hundreds of billions of instructions per second? These issues are unlikely to be central to the near-term future of programming, as smaller-scale asynchronous parallelism certainly will be. But they are fascinating and important nonetheless. The last four chapters each comment on the implications for massive parallelism of the program structures they present.

The other subsidiary focus is *coordination*, a term we explain below. In general, there are many reasons to build software in the form of multi-process ensembles. Achieving speedup through parallelism is only one. The last chapter discusses multi-process programs that are *not* for speedup.

Ultimately, the questions raised by coordinated software fall off the map of computer science altogether. After all, the world at large is a mere asynchronous ensemble of asynchronous ensembles. Sociological, economic, mechanical and biological systems can be approached in these terms. Human ensembles can be supported by some of the same software structures that process ensembles rely on. One way to treat the art and science of coordinated software is precisely as a microcosmic introduction to a much broader topic, the analysis of coordinated systems in general. Coordinated software is a laboratory for the study of how a single undertaking is synthesized out of many separate activities.

These broader issues are not the main point here. We discuss them only in the exercises. Hard-nosed software-engineering types are welcome to ignore them altogether. But readers who are willing to exercise their imaginations may find in this topic (as in massive parallelism) lots to think about.

The programming language. Parallel programming requires the use of a *computing language* and a *coordination language*. Broadly speaking, the *coordination language* is the glue that allows us to build a unified program out of many separate activities, each specified using a *computing language*. A computing language (Fortran, C, Lisp,...) allows us to compute values and manipulate local data objects; a coordination language must allow us to create simultaneous activities, and must allow those activities to communicate with each other. It's possible to subsume the functions of a standard computing language *and* a coordination language within a single all-in-one super-language. We prefer for many reasons to rely on a standard computing language plus a (separate) coordination language. In this book, the computing language we use is C; the coordination language is Linda. We assume familiarity with C but not with Linda. (Readers needn't be expert C programmers. It should be an easy transition from any Algol-based language—Pascal, etc.—to a level of expertise sufficient for this book.)

C and Linda jointly form a good basis for this book because they are powerful, simple, efficient languages that have been implemented on a wide range of machines. But this book is not *about* C or Linda, any more than a generic "Introductory Programming with Pascal" book is about Pascal. The techniques to be discussed are applicable in any language environment comparable in expressive power to the C-Linda combination.

1.2 Why?

Parallelism will become, in the not too distant future, an essential part of every programmer's repertoire. *Coordination*—a general phenomenon of which parallelism is one example—will become a basic and widespread phenomenon in computer science. Every programmer, software engineer and computer scientist will need to understand it. We discuss these claims in turn.

1.2.1 Parallelism

Parallelism is a proven way to run programs fast. Everybody who has an interest in running his programs fast has an interest in parallelism— whether he knows it or not.

The most powerful computer at any given time must, by definition, be a parallel machine. Once you have taken your best shot and built the fastest processor that current technology can support, two of them are faster. Now consider the intermediate and the bottom levels—roughly speaking, the level of time-shared computers or file servers, and of workstations and personal computers (these categories are rapidly fuzzing together, of course). Manufacturers are increasingly discovering that, having provided the basic hardware and software infrastructure for a computer—the devices, communication busses, power supply, terminal, operating system and so on—it doesn't necessarily make sense to stop at one processor. Adding more processors to the same box is often a highly efficient way to buy more power at low incremental cost.

First-generation parallel machines were generally aimed at the high-through-medium range of the market. Machines like the BBN Butterfly, Intel iPSC, Sequent Balance and Symmetry, Alliant FX/8, Encore Multimax, NCUBE and others belong in this category. More recent machines are often more powerful and relatively less expensive. This category includes (for example) new multiprocessors from Silicon Graphics, Hewlett Packard/Apollo and Zenith, machines based on the Inmos Transputer processor (from Meiko, Cogent, Chorus and others) and many more. In early 1990 the market is bracing for an onslaught of "parallel PC's," based on the Intel processors that IBM uses in its personal computer line. These are designed in the first instance as file servers for workstation networks. But no wide-awake observer has failed to notice that they will be good platforms for parallel applications too. Look for specialty software houses to start selling shrink-wrapped parallel applications for these machines within the next few years—graphics packages, math and statistics libraries, database searchers, financial and market models, fancy spreadsheets. (We'll say more about applications below.) Thereafter the big software houses will jump on the bandwagon, and parallelism will truly be "mainstream."

Now, forget about parallel computers. Computer networks are, perhaps, an even more important basis for parallelism.

Processors that are packed into a single box can usually communicate with each other at much greater speeds than processors connected in a local or wide-area network. Still, the principle is the same. We can take a hard problem, break it into pieces and hand one piece to each of n processors, whether the processors occupy one box or are strung out across the country. Some parallel programs that run well on parallel computers fail to perform well on networks. Many programs can be made to perform well in both kinds of environment. We'll discuss the issues in detail in the following chapters.

We'll start, again, at the high end. The argument is in essence the same as before. If you have a problem that is hard enough to defeat the fastest current-generation supercomputer (whether it's a parallel machine or not), your next step is a *network* of supercomputers. Clearly, the ultimate computing resource at any given time isn't the fastest supercomputer, it's *all* the fastest supercomputers—or as many as you can find on a single network—focussed simultaneously on one problem, acting in effect like a single parallel machine.

The typical modern office or lab environment—many workstations or personal computers, networked together—is another promising environment for parallelism, arguably the most promising of all. If you sum up total computing power over all nodes of a typical local area network, you often wind up with a significant power pool. The more powerful the nodes and the more of them, the greater the power reserve. Of course, the power pool is cut up into bite-sized desk-top chunks; the only way to get at the *whole thing* is to run a parallel program on many nodes simultaneously.

If there are times of day when most nodes are idle, we can treat these idle nodes as a temporary parallel computer. But even when most nodes are working, experience suggests that (on average) many of them aren't working very hard. Users who run compute-intensive problems also read their mail, edit files, think, flirt, fulminate, eat lunch, crumple up paper and toss it at the wastebasket and perform various other compute-unintensive activities. Let's say you're a medium-sized organization and you own a network of one hundred workstations or personal computers. Let's say your machines are busy during normal working hours half time, on average. The real busy-ness number may be a lot lower. But assuming an average busy-ness of one half, your organization is the proud owner of an (on average) fifty-processor parallel computer, during the working day. Congratulations. Note that, whenever your network expands or the workstations are upgraded, your power pool grows more formidable.

Sophisticated workstation users will want (and will get) software tools that allow them to run on unused cycles from all over the network. (Such tools are already entering the commercial market.) Once again, software houses will build applications. And these trends aren't by any means inconsistent with the eventual rise of parallel workstations. Each user may have a parallel computer on his desk; *whatever* his desktop machine, it can use the network as a sounding-board to amplify its own compute power. It can gather up unused cycles from all over the network and throw them at the task in hand. A parallel program (if it is well-designed) has this special "expandability" property that no sequential program does: the more processors you happen to have, the more you can throw at the problem.

But what will organizations do with their network power pools?—with parallel machines in general? Do we really need all of this power?

Yes.

New power is needed so that we can run current program types better and faster, and to support basically new types of software as well. Vastly more powerful machines will solve larger numerical problems in more detail and with greater accuracy, run better simulations of larger and more complex systems, produce more detailed and sophisticated scientific visualizations. Scientists and engineers will rely on these techniques to progress on problems like computational molecular dynamics, weather prediction and climate modelling, aerospace system design and a formidable list of others.

Of course, computational power-lust isn't restricted to science and engineering. Parallel machines will support sophisticated graphics and high-quality voice and handwriting recognition. The most important extra-scientific use of parallelism will probably center on databases: parallelism will support fast searches through huge piles of data using sophisticated search criteria. Further, parallelism will enormously expand the boundaries of what fits inside of "real time"—animation, "artificial reality," avionics will benefit; so will high-level monitor programs designed to sift through torrents of incoming data for significant patterns. There are many other examples. Some are discussed in the following chapters.

1.2.2   Coordination

Thus far, we've focussed on the first part of our claim: that parallelism will become an essential part of every programmer's repertoire. We now turn to the second: that *coordination*—a general phenomenon of which parallelism is one example—will become a central topic in computer science.

In studying parallelism, you are studying one kind of coordinated programming. (Many parallelism techniques are applicable *verbatim* to other kinds of coordinated applications.) In studying coordinated programming, you are studying a basic underpinning of all computing.

We use the term *coordination* to refer to the process of *building programs by gluing together active pieces*. Each "active piece" is a process, task, thread or any other locus of execution independent of the rest. (Executing "independently" means executing concurrently and asynchronously with the rest.) To "glue active pieces together" means to gather them into an ensemble in such a way that we can regard the ensemble itself as the program—all our glued-together pieces are in some sense working on the same problem. The "glue" must allow these independent activities to communicate and to synchronize with each other exactly as they need to. A *coordination language* provides this kind of glue.

Coordination is important conceptually because it can be treated as one of the two orthogonal axes that jointly span "software space." To have a useful computer system, you must have computation *and* coordination. Every computation must ultimately be connected to the outside world. *Connected to* entails *coordinated with*: the computer and its human user are two "active, independent pieces" that must be assembled into a coordinated ensemble if computation is to have any meaning.

This simple observation has several consequences. One way to view an operating system is precisely as an *ad hoc* coordination language. Any user-plus-computer is a coordinated ensemble, one special instance of the sort of thing that this book is about.

Further, the fact that a coordinated ensemble can include both software processes and human "processes" suggests the existence of a new species of software ("new" meaning not that examples are unknown, but that the species hasn't been mapped out and explored in general). We might call it "Turingware": processes and people encompassed within a single structure, knit together by ordinary coordinated-programming techniques. Within the ensemble, processes and people don't know whether they're dealing with other people or other processes[1].

Systems like the Unix command interpreter anticipate some aspects of "Turingware" when they allow terminal screens (thus ultimately human users) and ordinary files to be interchanged for some purposes. In full-blown Turingware, however, a human isn't a mere data terminus; he can be one node in a far-flung network. Certain modules of the system (to put things another way) are implemented by people. The goal is three-fold. First, to use the methods of parallel programming to build fast, flexible and powerful information-exchange frameworks (what we call coordination frameworks in later chapters) for human use. Second, to apply the architectural and organizational insights of parallel programming to the coordination of *human* ensembles. Third, to change software's status—to allow its seamless incorporation into human organizations, in such a way that a program may (for example) ask me for data, reach some conclusions and pass them along to other people. Human-type work gets done by humans, computer-type work is done

---

[1]The "Turing Test" for machine intelligence hinges on making people and processes indistinguishable beneath a uniform interface.

by "software robots," and they all work merrily together. Exercises in chapters 8 and 9 discuss some examples.

Operating system designers have always been concerned with coordination (under one name or another). Early work on parallel programming was heavily influenced by operating system design for exactly this reason. But coordination is becoming a phenomenon of increasing interest to programmers in general.

A *parallel program* and a *distributed system* are both coordinated programs. Parallel programs use concurrency to run fast; a distributed system—a distributed database, mail system or file service, for example—uses concurrent processes because of the *physical distribution* of the machines it manages. (A distributed mailer running on fifty workstations may encompass fifty separate processes, one per machine. But the point isn't to run fifty times faster than a one-machine mailer.)

The active pieces that make up a coordinated program may all be expressed on one language, or in many different languages. A coordinated program may, in other words, be a *language-heterogeneous* program.

The active pieces that make up a coordinated program may be separated either by space or by time. If two processes run at the same time on different machines, and the first needs to send information to the second, the information must be sent through space. But if two processes run on the *same* machine, one on Tuesday and the other on Thursday, we may have a logically identical coordination problem. The Tuesday process needs to send information to the Thursday process, only through time instead of through space. The result is, still, a coordinated program. "Time-wise" coordination languages usually take the the form of file systems or databases, and we are not used to thinking of "time-wise" process ensembles in the same way we think of space-wise ensembles. But the principles are the same. Readers will discover that many of the coordination techniques developed in the context of parallelism are logically applicable without modification to file-system or database problems as well.

In sum, coordination issues have always been fundamental to operating systems; and clearly they are central to parallel programming. But in the future, users will be tempted with increasing frequency and for all sorts of reasons to build large programs by gluing smaller ones together.

This approach complements a whole collection of current trends. Computer networks are ubiquitous; it's natural and desirable to treat them as *integrated* systems. It's quite clear that no single programming language is destined to predominate, that many languages will continue in use for the foreseeable future (and probably forever). Hitching mixed-language programs together is an increasingly obvious and desirable expedient. Special-purpose hardware is proliferating: if I have a graphics machine, a database server and a general-purpose "compute server," an application that requires all three services will run, naturally, on all three machines. And of course, the world's processor supply continues to explode. An environment in which processors are cheap and plentiful *demands* coordinated programming. In a world that has more processors at any given moment than it has running applications, a program that insists on staying holed up inside a single processor is going to look downright anti-social.

1.3   How?

Chapter two lays the conceptual basis for parallelism and coordination by presenting three basic paradigms for parallel programming. In chapter three we introduce Linda, and then present the basic programming techniques (particularly the basic *data structures* for coordination) that underlie all three fundamental approaches. Chapter four completes the groundwork by discussing debugging and performance measurement. In chapter five, the details come together: we show how to develop a simple parallel program under all three basic approaches.

Chapters six, seven and eight explore the three basic paradigms in greater detail. They focus on case studies of "real" applications, chapter six on a database problem, chapter seven on a matrix computation and chapter eight on a kind of network problem. Chapter nine discusses coordinated programming in the broader sense. It presents some classical coordination problems, and then discusses a distributed system. The appendix is a C-Linda programmer's manual.

The exercises, we emphasize, are an integral part of the text. Whether you plan to work through them or not, it makes no sense to read the book without reading the exercise sections. Programming students who have no access to a parallel computing environment might learn a great deal, we think, by doing these problems using a uniprocessor simulator. (If worst comes to worst, they can be treated as paper-and-pencil exercises.) Programming students who *do* have a parallel environment will emerge as *bona fide* parallel programmers if they pursue them seriously.

All the program examples and exercises are based on C-Linda, and the best way to approach this book is with a C-Linda implementation at hand. Implementations are available on a variety of parallel machines; a Linda simulator runs on a number of standard workstations[2]. But if you don't have Linda, can't get it or don't want it, there are other ways to approach this book. As we've noted, the programming problems can be treated as paper-and-pencil exercises. And the principles involved hold good in any language.

---

[2] C-Linda is distributed commercially by Scientific Computing Associates at 246 Church Street in New Haven, Connecticut. They can be reached at (203) 777-7442, or via netmail at linda@sca-sun.uucp.

2 Basic Paradigms for Coordination Frameworks

2.1 Introduction

How do we build programs using parallel algorithms? On a spectrum of approaches, three primary points deserve special mention. We can use *result parallelism*, *agenda parallelism* or *specialist parallelism*, terms we define. We refer to these three as the *basic paradigms* for parallelism. They establish three distinct ways of thinking about parallelism—of designing parallel programs, but also (for that matter) of analyzing parallelism wherever it occurs, even if the parallel actors are people or hardware instead of software.

Corresponding to these basic paradigms are three parallel *programming methods*—practical techniques for translating concepts into working programs. We can use message passing, distributed data structures or live data structures. Each programming method involves a different view of the role of processes and the distribution of data in a parallel program.

These basic paradigms and programming methods aren't provably the only ones possible. But empirically they cover all examples we have encountered in the research literature and in our own programming experience.

A *coordination framework* is the organizing strategy for a parallel program—the part of the program for which you rely in a coordination language. Our goal here is to explain the conceptual paradigms and the programming methods that apply to coordination frameworks, and the mapping between them.

2.2 Paradigms and methods

How to write parallel programs? For each paradigm there is a natural programming method; each method relates to the others in well-defined ways. (In other words, programs using method x can be transformed into programs using method y by following well-defined steps.) We will therefore develop the following approach to parallel programming:

> To write a parallel program, (1) choose the paradigm that is most natural for the problem, (2) write a program using the method that is most natural for that paradigm, and (3) if the resulting program isn't acceptably efficient, transform it methodically into a more efficient version by switching from a more-natural method to a more-efficient one.

First we explain the paradigms—result, agenda and specialist parallelism. Then we explain the methods: live data structures, distributed structures and message passing. Finally we discuss the relationship between concepts and methods, and give an example.

2.2.1   The paradigms

We can envision parallelism in terms of a program's *result*, a program's *agenda of activities* or of an *ensemble of specialists* that collectively constitute the program. We begin with an analogy.

Suppose you want to build a house. Parallelism—using many people on the job—is the obvious approach. But there are several different ways in which parallelism might enter.

First, we might envision parallelism by starting with the finished product, the *result*. The result can be divided into many separate components—front, rear and side walls, interior walls, foundation, roof and so on. After breaking the result into components, we might proceed to build all components simultaneously, assembling them as they are completed; we assign one worker to the foundation, one to the front exterior wall, one to each side wall and so on. All workers start simultaneously. Separate workers set to work laying the foundation, framing each exterior wall, building a roof assembly. They all proceed in parallel, up to the point where work on one component can't proceed until another is finished. In sum, each worker is assigned to *produce one piece of the result*, and they all work in parallel up to the natural restrictions imposed by the problem. This is the *result parallel* approach.

At the other end of the spectrum, we might envision parallelism by starting with the crew of workers who will do the building. We note that

house-building requires a collection of separate skills: we need surveyors, excavators, foundation-builders, carpenters, roofers and so on. We
assemble a construction crew in which each skill is represented by a separate specialist worker. They all start simultaneously, but initially most
workers will have to wait around. Once the project is well underway,
however, many skills (hence many workers) will be called into play simultaneously: the carpenter (building forms) and the foundation-builders
work together and concurrently, the roofer can be shingling while the
plumber is installing fixtures and the electrician is wiring, and so on.
Although a single carpenter does all the woodwork, many other tasks
will overlap and proceed simultaneously with his. This approach is particularly suited to *pipelined* jobs—jobs that require the production or
transformation of a series of identical objects. If we're building a group
of houses, carpenters can work on one house while foundation-builders
work on a second and surveyors on a third. But this strategy will often
yield parallelism even when the job is defined in terms of a single object,
as it does in the case of the construction of a single house. In sum, each
worker is assigned to *perform one specified kind of work*, and they all
work in parallel up to the natural restrictions imposed by the problem.
This is the *specialist parallel* approach.

Finally, we might envision parallelism in terms of an agenda of activities
that must be completed in building a house. We write out a list of
tasks; we assemble a collection of workers. Each worker grabs some task
and gets to work. When he's finished, he grabs another task. Workers
have no particular identities—no special commitment to any part of
the project. They do whatever needs doing. The *agenda of tasks* is in
control of the action: workers may need to consult it repeatedly. The
tasks on the agenda might occur in a single unordered collection (we tell
the workers "grab any task from this list"), or there might be a sequence
("first do all these tasks, then start on those"). We need a foundation
(foundation building might be represented by a collection of tasks on
the agenda); then we need a frame; then we need a roof; then we need
wallboard and perhaps plastering, and so on. We assemble a work team
of generalists, each member capable of performing any construction step.
First, everyone pitches in and builds the foundation; then, the same
group sets to work on the framing; then they build the roof; then some
of them work on plumbing while others (randomly chosen) do the wiring,

and so on. In sum, each worker is assigned to *pick a task from the agenda and do that task—and repeat, until the job is done*, and they all work in parallel up to the natural restrictions imposed by the problem. This is the *agenda parallel* approach.

The boundaries between the three paradigms can sometimes be fuzzy, and we will often mix elements of several paradigms in getting a particular job done. A specialist approach might make secondary use of agenda parallelism, for example, by assigning a team of workers to some specialty—the team of carpenters, for example, might execute the "carpentry agenda" in agenda-parallel style. It's nonetheless an essential point that *these three paradigms represent three clearly separate ways of thinking about the problem*:

> Result parallelism focuses on the shape of the finished product; specialist parallelism focuses on the make-up of the work crew; agenda parallelism focuses on the list of tasks to be performed.

We've talked about house building; our next (and final) topic is software. But the ubiquitous applicability of these paradigms to all sorts of human endeavors is thought provoking. We pursue this point in the exercises.

How do the three paradigms apply to software? Clearly

1. We can plan a parallel application around the data structure yielded as the ultimate result; we get parallelism by computing all elements of the result simultaneously.

2. We can plan an application around a particular agenda of tasks, and then assign many workers to execute the tasks.

3. We can plan an application around an ensemble of specialists connected into a logical network of some kind. Parallelism results from all nodes of the logical network (all the specialists) being active simultaneously.

How do we know what kind of parallelism—what paradigm—to use? Consider the house-building analogy again. In effect, all three classes are (or have been) used in building houses. Factory-built housing is assembled at the site using pre-built modules—walls, a roof assembly, staircases and so on; all these components were assembled separately and (in theory) simultaneously back at the factory. This is a form of result parallelism in action. "Barn raisings" evidently consisted of a group of workers turning its attention *en masse* to each element on a list of required tasks—a form of agenda parallelism. But some form of specialist parallelism, usually with secondary agenda parallelism, seems like the most natural choice for house-building: each worker (or team) has a specialty, and parallelism arises in the first instance when many separate specialities operate simultaneously, secondarily when the many (in effect) identical workers on one team cooperate on the agenda.

In software as well, certain paradigms tend to be more natural for certain problems. The choice depends on the problem to be solved. In some cases, one choice is immediate. In others, two or all three paradigms might be equally natural. This multiplicity of choices might be regarded as confusing or off-putting; we'd rather see it as symptomatic of the fact that parallelism is in many cases so abundant that the programmer can take his choice about how to harvest it.

In many cases, the easiest way to design a parallel program is to think of the resulting data structure—*result parallelism*. The programmer asks himself (1) is my program intended to produce some multiple-element data structure as its result (or can it be conceived in these terms)? If so, (2) can I specify exactly how each element of the resulting structure depends on the rest, and on the input? If so, it's easy (given knowledge of the appropriate programming methods) to write a result-parallel program. Broadly speaking, such a program reads as follows: "Build a data structure in such-and-such a shape; attempt to determine the value of all elements of this structure simultaneously, where the value of each element is determined by such-and-such a computation. Terminate when all values are known." It may be that the elements of the result structure are completely independent—no element depends on any other. If so, all computations start simultaneously and proceed in parallel. It may also be that some elements can't be computed until certain other values are known. In this case, all element-computations *start* simultaneously, but some immediately get stuck. They remain stuck until the values they rely on have been computed, and then proceed.

Consider a simple example: we have two n-element vectors, A and B, and need to compute their sum S. A result parallel program reads as follows: "Construct an n-element vector S; to determine the ith element of S, add the ith element of A to the ith element of B". The elements of S are completely independent. No addition depends on any other addition. All additions accordingly start simultaneously, and go forward in parallel.

More interesting cases involve computations in which there are dependencies among elements of the result data structure. We discuss an example in the next section.

Result parallelism is a good starting point for any problem whose goal is to produce a series of values with predictable organization and interdependencies, but not every problem meets this criterion. Consider a program that produces output whose shape and format depend on the input—a program to format text or translate code in parallel, for example, whose output may be a string of bytes and (perhaps) a set of tables, of unpredictable size and shape. Consider a program in which (conceptually) a *single* object is transformed repeatedly—an LU decomposition or linear programming problem, for example, in which a given matrix is repeatedly transformed in place. Consider a program that's executed not for value but for effect—a realtime monitor-and-control program, or an operating system, for example.

Agenda parallelism is a versatile approach that adapts easily to many different problems. The most flexible embodiment of this type of parallelism is the master-worker paradigm. In a master-worker program, a master process initializes the computation and creates a collection of identical worker processes. Each worker process is capable of performing any step in the computation. Workers seek a task to perform, perform the selected task and repeat; when no tasks remain, the program (or this step) is finished. The program executes in the same way no matter how many workers there are, so long as there is at least one. The same program might be executed with one, ten and 1000 workers in three consecutive runs. If tasks are distributed on the fly, this structure is naturally load-balancing: while one worker is tied up with a time-consuming task, another might execute a dozen shorter task assignments.

For example: suppose we have a database of employee records, and we need to identify the employee with (say) the lowest ratio of salary to dependents. Given a record Q, the function $r(Q)$ computes this ratio. The agenda is simple: "apply function r to all records in the database; return the identity of the record for which r is minimum." We can structure this application as a master-worker program in a natural way: the master fills a bag with data objects, each representing one employee record. Each worker repeatedly withdraws a record from the bag, computes r and sends the result back to the master. The master keeps track of the minimum-so-far, and when all tasks are complete, reports the answer.

Specialist parallelism involves programs that are conceived in terms of a logical network. They arise when an algorithm or a system to be modelled is best understood as a network in which each node executes a relatively autonomous computation, and inter-node communication follows predictable paths. The network may reflect a physical model, or the logical structure of an algorithm (as in a pipelined or systolic computation, for example). Network-style solutions are particularly transparent and natural when there is a physical system to be modelled. Consider a circuit simulator, for example, modelled by a parallel program in which each circuit element is realized by a separate process. There are also problems that partition naturally into separate realms of responsibility, with clearly-defined inter-communication channels; further on we discuss a "cooperating experts" type of heuristic monitor that uses this kind of organization. In chapter 5, we discuss a pipeline type of algorithm, an algorithm understood as a sequence of steps applied to a stream of input values, with each stage of the pipe transforming a datum and handing it forward.

For example: suppose a nation-wide trucking company needs to produce a large number of estimates for travel time between two points, given current estimates for road conditions, weather and traffic. We might design a specialist-parallel programs as follows: we embody a map of the continental U.S. in a logical network; each state is represented by its own node in the network. The Wyoming node is responsible for staying up-to-date on travel conditions in and expected transit time through Wyoming, and so forth. To estimate travel time from New Hampshire to Arkansas, we plan out a route, and include a representation of this route within a data object representing a truck. We hand the "truck" to New Hampshire, which estimates its travel time through New Hampshire

and then hands the truck to the next state along its route. Eventually
the "truck" reaches Arkansas, which prints out the final estimate for its
transit time. Note that large numbers of trucks may be moving through
the logical network at any one time.

We conclude this survey of paradigms by mentioning two special classes
that we won't deal with further, "data parallelism" and "speculative
parallelism" (sometimes called "or-parallelism"). Data parallelism is a
restricted kind of agenda parallelism: it involves a series of transformations each applied to all elements of a data structure simultaneously. If
we start with an agenda of activities in which each item requires that
a transformation be applied to a data structure, the agenda-parallel
program we'd derive would in effect be an example of data parallelism.
Empirically, data parallelism is usually associated with synchronous machines (e.g. MPP[Gil79], the Connection Machine[HS86]), and is accordingly tied to an implementation in which transformations are applied to all elements of some data structure not merely concurrently but
synchronously—at each instant, each active worker is applying the same
step of the same transformation to its own assigned piece of the structure. In this book, our focus is restricted to techniques that are used on
general-purpose *asynchronous* parallel machines [1].

In "speculative parallelism", often associated with logic programming
but also significant in (for example) parallel algorithms for heuristic
search (e.g. parallel alpha-beta search on game trees [MC82]), a collection of parallel activities is undertaken with the understanding that
some may ultimately prove to be unnecessary to the final result. Whenever a program's structure includes clauses like "try x, and if x fails,
try y" (and so on through a list of other alternatives), we can get parallelism by working on x, y and any other alternatives simultaneously.
If and when x fails, y is already underway. We understand this under
our schematization as another special form of agenda parallelism—many
workers are thrown simultaneously into the completion of a list of tasks,
with the understanding that ultimately, only one of the results produced
will be incorporated in the finished product.

---

[1] This focus can be taken as arbitrary, but there's a reason for it. At present
synchronous or SIMD machines are rare and expensive; asynchronous machines can
be built cheaply, and are increasingly widespread.

2.2.2   The programming methods

In message passing, we create many concurrent processes, and enclose
every data structure within some process; processes communicate by
exchanging messages. In message passing methods, no data objects are
shared among processes. Each process may access its own local set of
private data objects only. In order to communicate, processes must send
data objects from one local space to another; to accomplish this, the programmer must explicitly include send-data and receive-data operations
in his code (figure 2.1).

At the other extreme, we dispense with processes as conceptually-
independent entities, and build a program in the shape of the data
structure that will ultimately be yielded as the result. Each element
of this data structure is implicitly a separate process, which will turn
into a data object upon termination. To communicate, these implicit
processes don't exchange messages; they simply "refer" to each other as
elements of some data structure. Thus if process P has data for Q, it
doesn't send a message to Q; it terminates, yielding a value, and Q reads
this value directly. These are "live data structure" programs (figure 2.2).

The message passing and live data structure approaches are similar in the
sense that in each, all data objects are distributed among the concurrent
processes; there are no global, shared structures. In message passing,
though, processes are created by the programmer *explicitly*, they communicate *explicitly* and may send values *repeatedly* to other processes.
In a live data structure program, processes are created *implicitly* in the
course of building a data structure, they communicate *implicitly* by referring to the elements of a data structure, and each process produces
only a *single* datum for use by the rest of the program. Details will
become clear as we discuss examples.

Between the extremes of allowing all data to be absorbed into the process
structure (message passing) or all processes to melt into a data structure
(live data structures), there's an intermediate strategy that maintains
the distinction between a group of data objects and a group of processes.
Many processes share direct access to many data objects or structures.
Because shared data objects exist, processes may communicate and coordinate by leaving data in shared objects. These are "distributed data
structure" programs (figure 2.3).

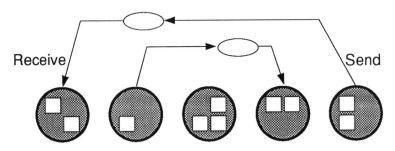

Figure 2.1
Message passing: the process structure—the number of processes and their
relationships—determines the program structure. A collection of concurrent
processes communicate by exchanging messages; every data object is locked inside
some process. (Processes are round, data objects square, messages oval.)

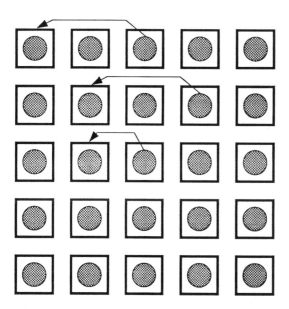

Figure 2.2
Live data structures: the *result data structure*—the number of its elements, and
their relationship—determines the program structure. Every concurrent *process* is
locked inside a data object—is responsible, in other words, for computing that
element and only that element. Communication is no longer a matter of explicit
"send message" and "receive message" operations; when a process needs to consult
the value produced by some other process, it *reads* the data object within which the
process is trapped.

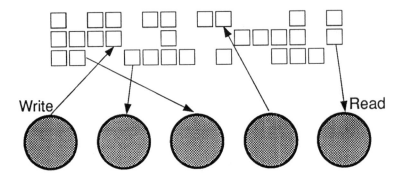

Figure 2.3
Distributed data structures: Concurrent processes *and* data objects figure as
autonomous parts of the program structure. Processes communicate by reading and
writing shared data objects.

2.3   Where to use each?

It's clear that result parallelism is naturally expressed in a live data structure program. For example: returning to the vector-sum program, the core of such an application is a live data structure. The live structure is an n element vector called S; trapped inside each element of S is a process that computes $A[i] + B[i]$ for the appropriate i. When a process is complete, it vanishes, leaving behind only the value it was charged to compute.

Specialist parallelism is a good match to message passing: we can build such a program under message passing by creating one process for each network node, and using messages to implement communication over edges. For example: returning to the travel-time program, we implement each node of the logical network by a process; trucks are represented by messages. To introduce a truck into the network at New Hampshire, we send New Hampshire a "new truck" message; the message includes a representation of the truck's route. New Hampshire computes an estimated transit time and sends another message, including both the route and the time-en-route-so-far, to the next process along the route. Note that, with lots of trucks in the network, many messages may converge on a process simultaneously. Clearly, then, we need some method for queuing or buffering messages until a process can get around to dealing with them. Most message passing systems have some kind of buffering mechanism built in.

Even when such a network model exists, though, message passing will sometimes be inconvenient in the absence of backup-support from distributed data structures. If every node in the network needs to refer to a collection of global status variables, those globals can only be stored (absent distributed data structures) as some node's local variables, forcing all access to be channeled through a custodian process. Such an arrangement can be conceptually inept and can lead to bottlenecks.

Agenda parallelism maps naturally onto distributed data structure methods. Agenda parallelism requires that many workers set to work on what is, in effect, a single job. In general, any worker will be willing to pick up any task. Results developed by one worker will often be needed by others, but one worker usually won't know (and won't care) what the others are doing. Under the circumstances, it's far more convenient to leave results in a distributed data structure, where any worker who wants them can take them, than to worry about sending messages to particular recipients. Consider also the dynamics of a master-worker program— the kind of program that represents the most flexible embodiment of agenda parallelism. We have a collection of workers and need to distribute tasks, generally on the fly. Where do we keep the tasks? Again, a distributed data structure is the most natural solution. If the tasks on the agenda are strictly parallel, with no necessary ordering among them, the master process can store task descriptors in a distributed *bag* structure; workers repeatedly reach into the bag and grab a task. In some cases, tasks should be started in a certain order (even if many can be processed simultaneously); in this case, tasks will be stored in some form of distributed queue or stream.

For example: we discussed a parallel database search carried out in terms of the master-worker model. The bag into which the master process drops employee records is naturally implemented as a distributed data structure—as a structure, in other words, that is directly accessible to the worker processes and the master.

2.4   An example

Consider a naive n-body simulator: on each iteration of the simulation, we calculate the prevailing forces between each body and all the rest, and update each body's position accordingly[2]. We'll consider this problem in the same way we considered house building. Once again, we can conceive of result-based, agenda-based and specialist-based approaches to a parallel solution.

We can start with a result-based approach. It's easy to restate the problem description as follows: suppose we're given n bodies, and want to run q iterations of our simulation; compute a matrix M such that $M[i, j]$ is the position of the ith body after the jth iteration. The zeroth column of the matrix gives the starting position, the last column the

---

[2] There is a better $(O(n))$ approach to solving the n-body problem, developed by Rokhlin and Greengard of Yale [GR87]; the new algorithm can be parallelized, but to keep things simple, we use the old approach as a basis for this discussion.

final position, of each body. We've now carried out step 1 in the design
of a live data structure. The second step is to define each entry in terms
of other entries. We can write a function *position(i, j)* that computes
the position of body *i* on iteration *j*; clearly, *position(i,j)* will depend
on the positions of each body at the previous iteration—will depend,
that is, on the entries in column *j-1* of the matrix. Given a suitable
programming language, we're finished: we build a program in which
$M[i, j]$ is defined to be the value yielded by *position(i,j)*. Each invocation
of *position* constitutes an implicit process, and all such invocations are
activated and begin execution simultaneously. Of course, computation
of the second column can't proceed until values are available for the
first column: we must assume that, if some invocation of *position* refers
to $M[x, y]$ and $M[x, y]$ is still unknown, we wait for a value, and then
proceed. Thus the zeroth column's values are given at initialization time,
whereupon all values in the first column can be computed in parallel,
then the second column and so forth (figure 2.4).

(Note that, if the forces are symmetric, this program does more work
than necessary, because the force between A and B is the same as the
force between B and A. This is a minor problem that we could correct,
but our goal here is to outline the simplest possible approach.)

We can approach this problem in terms of agenda parallelism also. The
task agenda states "repeatedly apply the transformation *compute next
position* to all bodies in the set". To write the program, we might create
a master process and have it generate n initial task descriptors, one for
each body. On the first iteration, each worker in a group of identical
worker processes repeatedly grabs a task descriptor and computes the
next position of the corresponding body, until the pile of task descriptors is used up (and all bodies have advanced to their new positions).
Likewise for each subsequent iteration. A single worker will require time
proportional to n^2 to complete each iteration; two workers together will
finish each iteration in time proportional to $n^2/2$, and so on. We can
store information about each body's position at the last iteration in a
distributed table structure, where each worker can refer to it directly
(figure 2.5).

Finally we might use a specialist-parallel approach: we create a series
of processes, each one specializing in a single body—that is, each responsible for computing a single body's current position throughout the

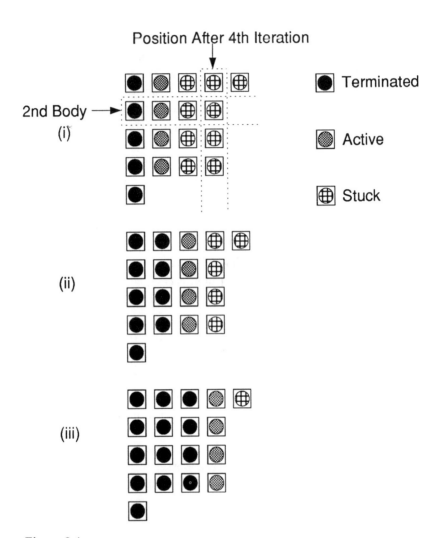

Figure 2.4
A live data structure approach to the n-body problem. To begin, we build an $n \times q$ matrix and install a process inside each element. The process trapped in element $M[i, j]$ will compute the position of the ith body after the jth iteration, by referring to the previous column, in which each body's last-known position will appear. The processes in column j are stuck until the processes in column $j - 1$ terminate, at which point all of column j can be computed in parallel. Thus each column computes in parallel until values are known for the entire matrix.

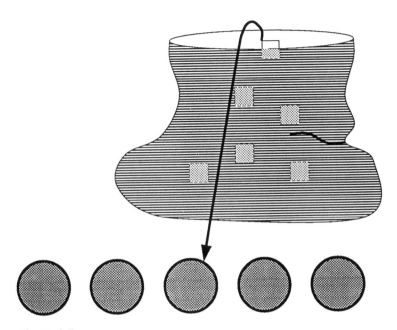

Figure 2.5
A distributed data structure version. At each iteration, workers repeatedly pull a
task out of a distributed bag and compute the corresponding body's new position,
referring to a distributed table for information on the previous position of each
body. After each computation, a worker might update the table (without erasing
information on previous positions, which may still be needed), or might send
newly-computed data to a master process, which updates the table in a single
sweep at the the end of each iteration.

simulation. At the start of each iteration, each process informs each other process by message of the current position of its body. All processes are behaving in the same way; it follows that, at the start of each iteration, each process *sends data to* but also *receives data from* each other process. The data included in the incoming crop of messages is sufficient to allow each process to compute a new position for its body. It does so, and the cycle repeats (figure 2.6). (A similar but slightly cleaned up—*i.e.*, more efficient—version of such a program is described by Seitz in [Sei85].)

2.5   A methodology: how do the three techniques relate?

The methodology we're developing requires (1) starting with a paradigm that is natural to the problem, (2) writing a program using the programming method that is natural to the paradigm, and then (3) if necessary, transforming the initial program into a more efficient variant that uses some other method. If a natural approach also turns out to be an efficient approach, then obviously no transformation is necessary. If not, it's essential to understand the relationships between the techniques and the performance implications of each. After describing the relationships in general, we discuss one case of this transformation-for-efficiency in some detail.

The relationships. The main relationships are shown in figure 2.7. Both live data structures and message passing center on *captive data objects*—every data object is permanently associated with some process. Distributed data structure techniques center on *delocalized* data objects, objects not associated with any one process, freely floating about on their own. We can transform a live data structure or a message passing program into a distributed structure program by using *abstraction*: we cut the data objects free of their associated processes and put them in a distributed data structure instead. Processes are no longer required to fix their attention on a single object or group of objects; they can range freely. To move from a distributed structure to a live data structure or a message passing program, we use *specialization*: we take each object and bind it to some process.

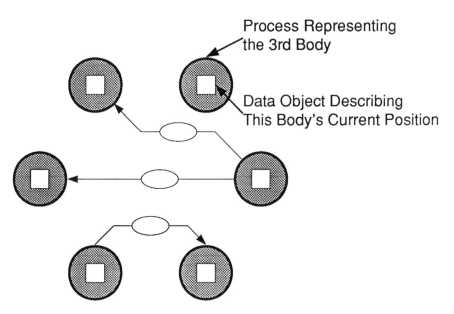

Figure 2.6
The message passing version. While the live-data-structure program creates nq processes (q was the number of iterations, and there are n bodies), and the distributed data structure program creates any number of workers it chooses, this message passing program creates exactly n processes, one for each body. In each of the other two versions, processes refer to *global data structures* when they need information on the previous positions of each body. (In the live data structure version, this global data structure was the "live" structure in which the processes themselves were embedded.) But in the message passing version, no process has access to any data object external to itself. Processes keep each other informed by sending messages back and forth.

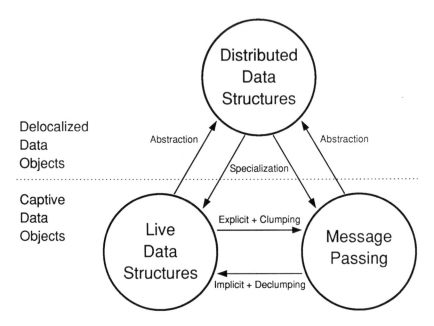

Figure 2.7
The game of parallelism.

It's clear from the foregoing that live data structures and message passing are strongly related, but there are also some important differences. To move from the former to the latter we need to make communication *explicit*, and we may optionally use *clumping*. A process in a live-data-structure program has no need to communicate information explicitly to any other process. It merely terminates, yielding a value. In a message passing program, a process with data to convey must execute an explicit "send message" operation. When a live-data-structure process requires a data value from some other process, it references a data structure; a message passing process will be required to execute an explicit "receive message" operation.

Why contemplate a move from live data structures to message passing, if the latter technique is merely a verbose version of the former? It's not; message passing techniques offer an added degree of freedom, which is available via "clumping". A process in a live-data-structure program develops a value and then dies. It can't live on to develop and publish another value. In message passing, a process can develop as many values as it chooses, and disseminate them in messages whenever it likes. It can develop a whole series of values during a program's lifetime. Hence "clumping": we may be able to let a single message passing process do the work of a whole collection of live-data-structure processes.

Using abstraction and then specialization to transform a live data structure program. Having described some transformations in the abstract, what good are they? We can walk many paths through the simple network in figure 2.7, and we can't describe them all in detail. We take up one significant case, describing the procedure in general and presenting an example; we close the section with a brief examination of another interesting case.

Suppose we have a problem that seems most naturally handled using result parallelism. We write the appropriate live data structure program, but it performs poorly, so we need to apply some transformations.

First, why discuss this particular case? When the problem is suitable, a live data structure program is likely to be rather easy to design and concise to express. It's likely to have a great deal of parallelism (with the precise degree depending, obviously, on the size of the result structure and the dependencies among elements). But it may also run poorly on most current-generation parallel machines, because the live-data-structure approach tends to produce *fine-grained* programs—programs that create a large number of processes, each one of which does relatively little computing. Concretely, if our resulting data structure is (say) a ten thousand element matrix, this approach will implicitly create ten thousand processes. There's no reason in theory why this kind of program can't be supported efficiently, but on most current parallel computers there are substantial overheads associated with creating and coordinating large numbers of processes. This is particularly true on distributed-memory machines, but even on shared-memory machines that support lightweight processes, the potential gain from parallelism can be overwhelmed by huge numbers of processes each performing a trivial computation.

If a live data structure program performs well, we're finished; if it doesn't, a more efficient program is easily produced by *abstracting* to a distributed data structure version of the same algorithm. We replace the live data structure with a passive one, and raise the processes one level in the conceptual scheme: each process *fills in* many elements, rather than *becoming* a single element. We might create one hundred processes, and have each process compute one hundred elements of the result. The resulting program is coarser-grained than the original—the programmer decides how many processes to create, and can choose a reasonable number. We avoid the overhead associated with huge numbers of processes.

This second version of the program may still not be efficient enough, however. It requires that each process read and write a single data structure, which must be stored in some form of logically shared memory. Accesses to a shared memory will be more expensive than access to local structures. Ordinarily this isn't a problem; distributed data structure programs can be supported efficiently even on distributed-memory (e.g., hypercube) machines. But for some communication-intensive applications, and particularly on distributed memory machines, we may need to go further in order to produce an efficient program. We might produce a maximally-efficient third version of the program by using *specialization* to move from distributed data structures to message passing. We break the distributed data structure into chunks, and hand each chunk to the process with greatest interest in that chunk. Instead of a shared distributed data structure, we now have a collection of local data structures, each encapsulated within and only accessible to a single process. When some process needs access to a "foreign chunk"—a part of the data structure that it doesn't hold locally—it must send a message to the process that does hold the interesting chunk, asking that an update be performed or a data value returned. This is a nuisance, and usually results in an ugly program. But it eliminates direct references to any shared data structures.

Under this scheme of things, we can see a neat and well-defined relationship among our three programming methods. We start with an elegant and easily-discovered but potentially inefficient solution using live data structures, move on via abstraction to a more efficient distributed data structure solution, and finally end up via specialization at a low-overhead message passing program. (We might alternatively have gone directly from live data structures to message passing via "clumping".)

There's nothing inevitable about this procedure. In many cases it's either inappropriate or unnecessary. It's inappropriate if live data structures are *not* a natural starting point. It's unnecessary if a live data structure program runs well from the start. It's partially unnecessary if abstraction leads to a distributed data structure program that runs well—in this case, there's nothing to be gained by performing the final transformation, and something to be lost (because the message passing program will probably be substantially more complicated than the distributed data structure version). It's also true that message passing programs are not always more efficient than distributed data structure versions; often they are, but there are cases in which distributed data structures are the optimal approach.

An example. For example, returning to the n-body simulator: we discussed a live-data structure version; we also developed distributed data structure and message passing versions, independently. We could have used the live-data structure version as a basis for abstraction and specialization as well.

Our live data structure program created $n \times q$ processes, each of which computed a single invocation of *position* and then terminated. We can create a distributed data structure program by *abstraction*. M is now a distributed data structure—a passive structure, directly accessible to all processes in the program. Its zeroth column holds the initial position of each body; the rest of the matrix is blank. We create k processes and put each in charge of filling in one band of the matrix. Each band is filled-in column-by-column. In filling-in the jth column, processes refer to the position values recorded in the j-$1st$ column. We now have a program in which number-of-processes is under direct programmer control; we can run the program with two or three processes if this seems reasonable (as it might if we have only two or three processors available). We've achieved lower process-management overheads, but the new program was easy to develop from the original, and will probably be only slightly less concise and comprehensible.

Finally we can use *specialization* to produce a minimal-overhead message passing program. Each process is given one band of M to store in its own local variable space; M no longer exists as a single structure. Since processes can no longer refer directly to the position values computed on the last iteration, these values must be disseminated in messages. At the end of each iteration, processes exchange messages; messages hold the positions computed by each process on the last iteration. We've now achieved low process-management overhead, and also eliminated the overhead of referring to a shared distributed data structure. But the cost is considerable: the code for this last version will be substantially more complicated and messier than the previous one, because each process will need to conclude each iteration with a message-exchange operation in which messages are sent, other messages are received and local tables are updated. We've also crossed an important conceptual threshold: communication in the first two solutions was conceived in terms of *references to data structures*, a technique that is basic to all programming. But the last version relies on message passing for communication—thus substituting a new kind of operation that is conceptually in a different class from standard programming techniques.

When to abstract and specialize? How do we know whether we need to use abstraction, or to move onward to a message passing program? The decision is strictly pragmatic; it depends on the application, the programming system and the parallel machine. Consider one concrete datum: using C-Linda on current parallel machines, specialization leading to a message passing program is rarely necessary. Most problems have distributed data structure solutions that perform well. In this context, though, abstraction to a distributed data structure program usually *is* necessary to get an efficient program.

Another path through the network: abstraction from message passing When live-data-structure solutions are natural, they may involve too many processes and too much overhead, so we use abstraction to get a distributed data structure program. It's also possible for a message passing, network-style program to be natural, but to involve too many processes and too much inter-process communication—in which case we can use abstraction, again, to move from *message passing* to distributed data structures. Suppose, for example, that we want to simulate a ten thousand element circuit. It's natural to envision one process for each circuit element, with processes exchanging messages to simulate the propagation of signals between circuit elements. But this might lead to a high-overhead program that runs poorly. Abstraction, again, allows us to create fewer processes and put each in charge of one segment of a distributed data structure that represents the network state as a whole.

In sum, there are many paths that a programmer might choose to walk though the state diagram in figure 2.7. But the game itself is simple: start at whatever point is most natural, write a program, understand its performance and then, if necessary, follow the "efficiency" edges until you reach an acceptable stopping place.

2.6 Where are the basic techniques supported?

Although it's our intention in this book to discuss programming techniques, not programming systems, a brief guide to the languages and systems in which the basic techniques occur may be helpful.

Before we discuss some possibilities from the programming methodology point of view, we need to address the basic character of these proposals. The bulk of published work on languages and systems for parallelism deals with *integrated parallel or distributed programming languages* or with *operating systems* that support parallel or distributed programming. Linda, on the other hand, is a *coordination language*. The distinction is important. An integrated parallel language is a complete, new programming language with built-in support for coordination. An *operating system* that supports coordination isn't (of course) a language at all. It supplies a collection of utility routines (to perform message passing, for example) to be invoked by user programs in the same way that I/O or math-library routines might be invoked. These routines get no (or essentially no) compiler support. A *coordination language* *is* a language, but one that embodies a coordination model *only*. A new compiler (for example, a C-Linda compiler) supports a *combined* language environment, consisting of a computing language plus a coordination language.

There are relatively few coordination languages on the market, but Linda isn't the only one. Dongarra and Sorenson's Schedule [DSB88] is another

example. Schedule in turn is related to Babb's work on coarse-grain
dataflow [Bab84]. Strand is an example that approaches the problem
from a logic-programming viewpoint [FT89]. We expect to see many
more examples in coming years.

Message passing is by far the most widespread of the basic models; it occurs in many different guises and linguistic contexts. The best-known of
message passing languages is Hoare's influential fragment CSP [Hoa78],
which inspired a complete language called occam [May83]. CSP and
occam are based on a radically tight-knit kind of message passing: both
the sending and the receiving of a message are *synchronous* operations.
A process with a message to send blocks until the designated receiver has
taken delivery. CSP and occam are *static* languages as well: they don't
allow new processes to be created dynamically as a program executes.
CSP and occam are for these reasons not expressive enough to support
the full range of message-passing-type programs we discuss here.

Monitor and remote-procedure-call languages and systems are another
subtype within the message passing category (with a qualification we
note below). In these systems, communication is modelled on procedure
call: one process communicates with another by invoking a procedure
defined within some other process or within a passive, globally-accessible
module. This kind of quasi-procedure-call amounts to a specialized form
of message passing: arguments to the procedure are shipped out in one
message, results duly returned in another. The qualification mentioned
above is that, in certain cases, systems of this sort are used for quasi-
distributed data structure programs. A global data object can be encapsulated in a module, then manipulated by remotely-invoked procedures.
(The same kind of thing is possible in any message passing system,
but it's more convenient given a procedure-style communication interface.) Why *quasi*-distributed data structures? As we understand the
term, a distributed data structure is directly accessible to many parallel
processes *simultaneously*. (Clearly we may sometimes need to enforce
sequential access to avoid corrupting data, but in general many read
operations may go forward simultaneously, and many write operations
that affect separate and independent parts of the same structure may
also proceed simultaneously – for example, many independent writes
to separate elements of a single matrix.) Languages in this class support data objects that are global to many processes, but in general they

allow processes one-at-a-time access only. Nor do they support plain distributed data objects; a global object must be packaged with a set of access procedures.

Monitors were first described by Hoare [Hoa74], and they have been used as a basis for many concurrent programming languages—for example Concurrent Pascal [Bri75], Mesa [LR80], Modula [Wir77]. (A *concurrent* language, unlike a parallel language, assumes that multiple processes inhabit the same address space.) Fairly recently they have been revived for use in parallel programming, in the form of parallel object-oriented programming languages (*e.g.* Emerald [JLHB88]. A form of remote procedure call underlies Ada [Ada82]; Birrell and Nelson's RPC kernel [BN84] is an efficient systems-level implementation.

Another variant of message passing centers on the use of *streams*: senders (in effect) append messages to the end of a message stream; receivers inspect the stream's head. This form of communication was first proposed by Kahn [Kah74], and it forms the basis for communication in most concurrent logic languages (e.g. Concurrent Prolog [Sha87], Parlog [Rin88]) and in functional languages extended with constructs for explicit communication (e.g. [Hen82]).

Message passing of one form another appears as a communication method in many other parallel languages (for example in Poker [Sny90]) and in many operating systems: for example the V kernel [CZ85], Mach [You87], Amoeba [MT86].

Distributed data structures are less frequently encountered. The term was introduced in the context of Linda [CGL86]. Distributed data structures form the *de facto* basis of a number of specialized Fortrans that revolve around parallel do-loops, for example Jordan's Force system [Jor86]. In this kind of system, parallelism is created mainly by specifying parallel loops—loops in which iterations are executed simultaneously instead of sequentially. Separate loop-iterations communicate through distributed structures that are adaptations of standard Fortran structures. Distributed data structures in one form of another are central in Dally's CST [Dal88], Bal and Tanenbaum's Orca [BT87] and Kale's Chare Kernel [Kal89], Browne's CODE[Bro90] and are supported in in Multilisp [Hal85] as well.

Live data structures are a central technique in several languages that support so-called non-strict data structures—data structures that can be accessed before they are fully defined. Id Nouveau [NPA86], Multilisp and Symmetric Lisp [GJL87] are examples. This same idea forms the implicit conceptual basis for the large class of functional languages intended for parallel programming (for example Sisal [LSF88] or Crystal [Che86]). Programs in these languages consist of a series of equations specifying values to be bound to a series of names. One equation may depend on the values returned by other equations in the set; we can solve all equations simultaneously, subject to the operational restriction that an equation referring to a not-yet-computed value can't proceed until this value is available. The equivalent program in live-data-structure terms would use each equation to specify the value of one element in a live data structure.

2.7 Exercises

The following is the only exercise set that doesn't involve programming. It's somewhat quirky, and not typical of the others. It can serve either as a basis for informal discussion or as a standard question set.

Other exercise sets include an occasional "general coordination" question along these lines too; when they occur in other chapters, they are marked out by a prefixed □ .

The paradigms we've discussed in this chapter are by no means limited to software. *Virtually all human organizations and virtually all machines* use parallelism. We can analyze the sorts of parallelism they use in exactly the same terms we've used for software structures.

Why would we want to do this? Does it do any good to identify one house-building technique as "result" and another as "agenda" parallelism? Perhaps. There are two sorts of potential benefit.

First, this kind of identification may be a useful way to develop and solidify the *mental models* (or the "intuitions") that underlie the programmer's approach to parallelism. Mental models are crucially important in our approach to programming (as to any other machine-building activity). Consider the quasi-physical model that underlies most programmer's idea of a "pushdown stack"—the model or mental picture of a heap of objects, with new objects added to and removed from the top. The physical model makes it easier for beginners to understand what stacks are. It continues in many cases to be useful to expert programmers as they conduct a mental search for the right data structure. Not every programmer relies on quasi-physical models, of course. But in our observation, many of the best and most creative programmers do. Building analogies between software structures and "real" structures is useful insofar as it promotes the formation of this kind of mental imagery.

There may be another benefit as well. Is there such a thing as the science of coordination?—the study of asynchronous systems in general? Such a study would attempt to characterize *in general* the trade-offs between (say) result- and specialist-parallelism, whether the systems at issue were biological, economic, software or whatever. It would attempt to use software (that most plastic, most easily-worked medium for machine-building) as a laboratory for the study of coordination phenomena, but it would also be willing to transfer good coordination strategies from (say) biological to economic domains.

The authors can't say for sure whether such a science exists or not. (Those who are interested in its potential existence should read Thomas Malone's "What is Coordination Theory," [Mal88]; they should probably consult Norbert Wiener's *Cybernetics* [Wie48] too, while they are at it.) If such a science *does* exist—if these sorts of investigations do prove *fruitful* and not merely interesting— the study of basic paradigms for coordination frameworks will have a significant role to play in it.

1. Human physiology and most internal-combustion engines rely on specialist *and* (in a sense) on agenda parallelism. Give examples and explain.

2. A nineteenth century German businessman noted (uneasily) that "... the incredibly elaborate division of labour diminish[es] the strength and intelligence which is required among the masses... [cited by Hobsbawm, Hobs69 p.65]" Translate this into software terms: in what sense does specialist parallelism lead to simpler, less-capable processes than agenda parallelism? But this argument is in some sense counter-intuitive— informally, "specialists" are often assumed to be *more* capable than non-specialists. Are there two species of specialist parallelism?

3. A simple result in electronics states the following: when we connect

two resistors in series, the total resistance is the sum of the individual resistances. When we connect them in parallel, the combined resistance is $\frac{R_1 R_2}{R_1 + R_2}$, there R_1 and R_2 are the values of the two resistances. The formula for resistors in parallel becomes simple and intuitive when we express it in terms of *conductance,* which is the reciprocal of resistance. When we connect resistors in parallel, their combined *conductance* is equal to the sum of the individual conductances. (For a discussion, see for example [HH80].)

Now, consider a collection of software processes of unequal capabilities: some work faster than others (perhaps because some are running on faster computers than others). We can build a specialist-parallel program (specifically a pipeline program) by connecting processes in series; we can build an agenda-parallel program (specifically a master-worker program, with dynamic task assignment) by connecting the processes in parallel. (*a*) Explain. (*b*) Define "software resistance" (or "conductance") in such a way that we can characterize the behavior of these two software structures using the same expressions that describe the electronics.

4. Harpsichord and organ engineers typically rely both on specialist and on agenda parallelism ("agenda" again in the broader sense we used above). Piano builders restrict themselves to agenda parallelism. Explain.

5. In what sense can we describe a coral reef, a city or a human vascular system as the products of result parallelism? In what sense can we describe a typical military assault against entrenched defenders in these terms? Again, we're using a somewhat more general understanding of the result paradigm. Explain.

6. Pipeline programs represent one version of specialist parallelism. Pipelines have several characteristics; the linear arrangement of their process graphs is only one. Describe a subset of specialist parallelism that includes pipelined programs as one instance, but also includes programs with non-linear process graphs. State as precisely as possible what characteristics a problem should have in order to profit from this style of solution.

7. Malone [Mal88, p. 8] writes that "several organizational theorists have identified a tradeoff between coordination and 'slack resources.'

Organizations with slack resources (such as large inventories or long product development times) can use them as a 'cushion' to reduce the need for close coordination." On the other hand, some American companies have adopted the Japanese "just in time" manufacturing system, in which inventories are minimal or non-existent, and a steady parade of delivery trucks supplies parts to a factory exactly when they are needed. Clearly both approaches have advantages. What are the software-structure analogs of these two alternatives?

3 Basic Data Structures

We've discussed paradigms and programming methods. We turn now to the practical question: how do we build working parallel programs? In this section we sketch implementations of the pieces out of which parallel programs are constructed.

We will start with a systematic investigation of distributed data structures. We will give an overview of the most important kinds of distributed structures, when each is used and how each is implemented. This first part of the discussion should equip readers with a reasonable tool-kit for building distributed data structure programs. Of course, we intend to discuss all three programming methods. But the other two are easily derived from a knowledge of distributed data structures, as we discuss in the following sections. We arrive at message-passing by restricting ourselves to a small and specialized class of distributed structures. We arrive at live-data-structures by building distributed structures out of processes instead of passive data objects.

We start with an overview of our coordination language. (C-Linda is described in greater detail in the appendix.)

3.1 Linda

Linda consists of a few simple operations that embody the "tuple space" model of parallel programming. A base language with the addition of these tuple-space operations yields a parallel-programming dialect. To write parallel programs, programmers must be able to create and coordinate multiple execution threads. Linda is a model of process creation and coordination that is *orthogonal* to the base language in which it's embedded. The Linda model doesn't care *how* the multiple execution threads in a Linda program compute what they compute; it deals only with how these execution threads (which it sees as so many black boxes) are created, and how they can be organized into a coherent program. The following paragraphs give a basic introduction. Linda is discussed in greater detail, and contrasted with a series of other approaches, in [CG89].

The Linda model is a *memory* model. Linda memory (called *tuple space*) consists of a collection of logical tuples. There are two kinds of tuples. Process tuples are under active evaluation; data tuples are passive. The process tuples (which are all executing simultaneously) exchange data by generating, reading and consuming data tuples. A process tuple that is finished executing turns into a data tuple, indistinguishable from other data tuples.

It's important to note that *Linda is a model, not a tool*. A *model* (or *paradigm*) represents a particular way of thinking about a problem. It can be *realized* (or *instantiated* or *implemented*) in many different ways and in many different contexts. A software *tool*, on the other hand, is a working system that can be used to solve problems. We will be discussing a system called C-Linda, which is a tool—a piece of software that supports parallel programming. C-Linda is one *realization* of the Linda model. There are many other realizations, and these others aren't necessarily compatible with (needn't even closely resemble) C-Linda.

Some realizations are designed as platforms for operating systems; they include multiple tuple spaces, and place restrictions on tuple format in the interests of efficiency in the absence of compiler support [Lel90]. Others, in a Lisp environment, replace Linda's matching protocol with Prolog-style unification [AJ89]. Others use Linda-style operations to supply blackboard-style communication within Prolog [ACD90]. Others treat Linda's idea of a tuple as an extension to a Pascal-style type system [BHK88]. Others integrate Linda into an object-oriented environment [MK88]; and there are many other projects ongoing, designed to build Linda-like systems for databases, for image-processing, for visualization, in many different Lisp and Prolog environments, and so on.

To summarize: Scheme and Common Lisp differ dramatically, but they're both realizations of the *Lisp* paradigm; Simula 67, Smalltalk and C++ differ even more radically, but they're all realizations of *object-oriented programming*. The C-Linda we discuss in this book is one realization of the Linda paradigm.

C-Linda has four basic tuple-space operations, `out`, `in`, `rd` and `eval`, and two variant forms, `inp` and `rdp`.

out(t) causes tuple t to be added to tuple space; the executing process continues immediately. A tuple is a series of typed values, for example

```
("a string", 15.01, 17, x),
```

or

```
(0, 1).
```

in(s) causes some tuple t that matches anti-tuple s to be withdrawn from tuple space. An anti-tuple is a series of typed fields; some are values (or "actuals"), others are typed place-holders (or "formals"). A formal is prefixed with a question mark. For example,

```
("a string", ? f, ? i, y).
```

The first and last field are *actuals*; the middle two fields are *formals*. Once in(s) has found a matching t, the values of the actuals in t are assigned to the corresponding formals in s, and the executing process continues. If no matching t is available when in(s) executes, the executing process suspends until one is, then proceeds as before. If many matching ts are available, one is chosen arbitrarily.

rd(s) is the same as in(s), with actuals assigned to formals as before, except that the matched tuple remains in tuple space.

Predicate versions of in and rd, inp and rdp, attempt to locate a matching tuple and return 0 if they fail; otherwise they return 1, and perform actual-to-formal assignment as described above. (If and only if it can be shown that, irrespective of relative process speeds, a matching tuple must have been added to tuple space before the execution of inp or rdp, and cannot have been withdrawn by any other process until the inp or rdp is complete, the predicate operations are *guaranteed* to find a matching tuple.)

eval(t) is the same as out(t), except that t is evaluated after rather than before it enters tuple space; eval implicitly creates one new process to evaluate each field of t. When all fields have been completely

evaluated, t becomes an ordinary passive tuple, which may be ined or
read like any other tuple.

A tuple exists independently of the process that created it, and in fact
many tuples may exist independently of many creators, and may collectively form a data structure in tuple space. It's convenient to build
data structures out of tuples because tuples are referenced associatively,
somewhat like the tuples in a relational database.

Examples: executing the out statements

```
out("a string", 15.01, 17, x)
```

and

```
out(0, 1)
```

causes the specified tuples to be generated and added to tuple space. An
in or rd statement specifies a template for matching: any values included
in the in or rd must be matched identically; formal parameters must be
matched by values of the same type. (It's also possible for formals to
appear in tuples, in which case a matching in or rd must have a type-
consonant value in the corresponding position.) Consider the statement

```
in("a string", ? f, ? i, y)
```

Executing this statement causes a search of tuple space for tuples of
four elements, first element "a string", last element equal to the value
bound to y, and middle two elements of the same types as variables f
and i respectively. When a matching tuple is found it is removed, the
value of its second field is assigned to f and its third field to i. The read
statement, for example

```
rd("a string", ? f, ? i, y)
```

works in the same way, except that the matched tuple is not removed. The values of its middle two fields are assigned to f and i as before, but the tuple remains in tuple space.

A tuple created using eval resolves into an ordinary data tuple. Consider the statement

```
eval("e", 7, exp(7)).
```

It creates a three-element "live tuple", and continues immediately; the live tuple sets to work computing the values of the string "e", the integer 7 and the function call exp(7). The first two computations are trivial (they yield "e" and 7); the third ultimately yields the value of e to the seventh power. Expressions that appear as arguments to eval inherit bindings from the environment of the eval-executing process *only* for whatever names they cite explicitly. Thus, executing eval("Q", f(x,y)) implicitly creates two new processes, which evaluate "Q" and f(x,y) respectively. The process evaluating f(x,y) does so in a context in which the names f, y and x have the same values they had in the environment of the process that executed eval. The names of any variables that happen to be free in f, on the other hand, were *not* cited explicitly by the eval statement, and no bindings are inherited for them. The statement

```
rd("e", 7, ? value))
```

might be used to read the tuple generated by the previous eval, once the live tuple has resolved to a passive data tuple—*i.e.*, once the necessary computing has been accomplished. (Executed before this point, it blocks until the active computation has resolved into a passive tuple.)

3.2   The basic distributed data structures

We can divide conventional "undistributed" data structures into three categories: (1) structures whose elements are identical or indistinguishable, (2) structures whose elements are distinguished by name, (3) structures whose elements are distinguished by position. It's useful to subdivide the last category: (3a) structures whose elements are "random-accessed" by position, (3b) structures whose elements are accessed under some ordering.

In the world of sequential programming, the first category is unimportant. A *set* of identical or indistinguishable elements qualifies for inclusion, but such objects are rare in sequential programming. Category 2 includes records, objects instantiated from class-definitions, sets and multi-sets with distinguishable elements, associative memories, Prolog-style assertion collections and other related objects. Category 3a consists mainly of arrays and other structures stored in arrays, 3b includes lists, trees, graphs and so on. Obviously the groupings aren't disjoint, and there are structures that can claim membership in several.

The distributed versions of these structures don't always play the same roles as their sequential analogs. Furthermore, factors with no conventional analogs can play a major role in building distributed structures. *Synchronization* concerns arising from the fact that a distributed structure is accessible to many asynchronous processes simultaneously form the most important example. Notwithstanding, every conventional category has a distributed analog.

3.3   Structures with identical or indistinguishable elements.

The most basic of distributed data structures is a lock or semaphore. In Linda, a counting semaphore is precisely a collection of identical elements. To execute a V on a semaphore `"sem"`,

```
out("sem");
```

to execute a P,

```
in("sem")
```

To initialize the semaphore's value to n, execute `out("sem")` n times. Semaphores aren't heavily used in most parallel applications (as opposed to most concurrent systems), but they do arise occasionally; we elaborate in the next section.

A *bag* is a data structure that defines two operations: "add an element" and "withdraw an element". The elements in this case needn't be identical, but they are treated in a way that makes them indistinguishable. Bags are unimportant in sequential programming, but extremely important to parallel programming. The simplest kind of replicated-worker program depends on a bag of tasks. Tasks are added to the bag using

```
out("task", TaskDescription)
```

and withdrawn using

```
in("task", ? NewTask)
```

Suppose we want to turn a conventional loop, for example

```
for ( <loop control> )
  <something>
```

into a parallel loop—all instances of *something* execute simultaneously. This construct is popular in parallel Fortran variants. One simple way to do the transformation has two steps. First we define a function `something()` that executes one instance of the loop body and returns, say, 1. Then we rewrite the loop:

```
for ( <loop control> )
  eval("this loop", something(<iteration-specific arg>));
for ( <loop control> )
  in("this loop", 1);
```

We have, first, created n processes; each is an active tuple that will resolve, when the function call `something()` terminates, to a passive tuple of the form `("this loop", 1)`. Second, we collect the n passive result tuples. These n may be regarded as a bag, or equivalently as a single counting semaphore which is V'ed implicitly by each process as it terminates. A trivial modification to this example would permit each iteration to "return" a result.

Name-accessed structures   Parallel applications often require access to a collection of related elements distinguished by name. Such a collection resembles a Pascal `record` or a C `struct`. We can store each element in a tuple of form

(name, value)

To read such a "record field", processes use `rd(name, ?  val)`; to update it,

in(name, ? old);
out(name, new)

As always, the synchronization characteristics of distributed structures distinguish them from conventional counterparts. Any process attempting to read a distributed record field while it is being updated will block until the update is complete and the tuple is reinstated. Processes occasionally need to wait until some event occurs; Linda's associative matching makes this convenient to program. For example, some parallel applications rely on "barrier synchronization": each process within some group must wait at a barrier until all processes in the group have reached the barrier; then all can proceed. If the group contains n processes, we set up a barrier called `barrier-37` by executing

out("barrier-37", n)

Upon reaching the barrier point, each process in the group executes (under one simple implementation)

```
in("barrier-37", ? val);
out("barrier-37", val-1);
rd("barrier-37", 0)
```

That is: each process decrements the value of the field called `barrier-37`, and then waits until its value becomes 0.

Position-accessed structures Distributed arrays are central to parallel applications in many contexts. They can be programmed as tuples of the form (*Array name, index fields, value*). Thus (`"V"`, 14, 123.5) holds the the fourteenth element of vector V; (`"A"`, 12, 18, 5, 123.5) holds one element of the three-dimensional array A, and so forth. For example: one way to multiply matrices A and B, yielding C, is to store A and B as a collection of rectangular blocks, one block per tuple, and to define a task as the computation of one block of the product matrix. Thus A is stored in tuple space as a series of tuples of the form

```
("A", 1, 1, <first block of A>)
("A", 1, 2, <second block of A>)
...
```

and B likewise. Worker processes repeatedly consult and update a *next-task* tuple, which steps though the product array pointing to the next block to be computed. If some worker's task at some point is to compute the i,jth block of the product, it reads all the blocks in A's *ith* row band and B's *jth* column band, using a statement like

```
for (next=0; next<ColBlocks; next++)
  rd("A", i, next, ? RowBand[next])
```

for A and similarly for B; then, using `RowBand` and `ColBand`, it computes the elements of C's i,jth block, and concludes the task step by executing

```
out("C", i, j, Product)
```

Thus "C" is a distributed array as well, constructed in parallel by the worker processes, and stored as a series of tuples of the form

```
("C", 1, 1, <first block of C>)
("C", 1, 2, <second block of C>).
```

It's worth commenting at this point on the obvious fact that a programmer who builds this kind of matrix multiplication program is dealing with two separate schemes for representing his data, the standard array structures of his base language and a tuple-based array representation. It would be simple in theory to demote the tuple-based representation to the level of assembler language generated by the compiler: let the compiler decide which arrays are accessed by concurrent processes, and must therefore be stored in tuple space; then have the compiler generate the appropriate Linda statements. Not hard to do—but would this be desirable?

We tend to think not. First, there are distributed data structures with no conventional analogs, as we've noted; a semaphore is the simplest example. It follows that parallel programmers won't be able to rely exclusively on conventional forms, and will need to master some new structures regardless of the compiler. But it's also the case that the dichotomy between *local memory* and *all other memory* is emerging as a fundamental attribute (arguably *the* fundamental attribute) of parallel computers. Evidence suggests that programmers can't hope to get good performance on parallel machines without grasping this dichotomy and allowing their programs to reflect it. This is an obvious point when applied to parallel architectures without physically-shared memory. Processors in such a machine have much faster access to data in their local memories then to data in another processor's local memory—non-local data is accessible only via the network and the communication software. But hierarchical memory is also a feature of shared-memory architectures. Thus an observation like the following, which deals with the BBN Butterfly shared-memory multiprocessor:

[A]lthough the Uniform System [a BBN-supplied parallel programming environment] provides the illusion of shared memory, attempts to use it as such do not work well. Uniform System programs that have been optimized invariably block-copy their operands into local memory, do their computation locally, and block-copy out their results... This being the case, it might be wise to optimize later-generation machines for very high bandwidth transfers of large blocks of data rather than single-word reads and writes as in the current Butterfly. We might end up with a computational model similar to that of LINDA [...], with naming and locking subsumed by the operating system and the LINDA **in,** **read** and **out** primitives implemented by very high speed block transfer hardware [Ols86].

Because the dichotomy between local and non-local storage appears to be fundamental to parallel programming, programmers should (we believe) have a high-level, language-based model for dealing with non-local memory. Tuple space provides such a model.

Returning to position-accessed distributed data structures: synchronization properties can again be significant. Consider a program to compute all primes between 1 and n (we examine several versions of this program in detail in chapter 5). One approach requires the construction of a distributed table containing all primes known so far. The table can be stored in tuples of the form

```
("primes", 1, 2)
("primes", 2, 3)
("primes", 3, 5)
. . .
```

A worker process may need the values of all primes up to some maximum; it reads upwards through the table, using **rd** statements, until it has the values it needs. It may be the case, though, that certain values are still missing. If all table entries through the kth are needed, but currently the table stops at j for $j < k$, the statement

```
rd("primes", j + 1, ? val)
```

blocks – there is still no $j + 1st$ element in the table. Eventually the $j + 1st$ element will be computed, the called-for tuple will be generated and the blocked **rd** statement unblocks. Processes that read past the end of the table will simply pause, in other words, until the table is extended.

Ordered or linked structures make up the second class of position-accessed data structures. It's possible to build arbitrary structures of this sort in tuple space; instead of linking components by address, we link by logical name. If C, for example, is a *cons* cell linking A and B, we can represent it as the tuple

```
("C", "cons", cell),
```

where **cell** is the two-element array **["A", "B"]**. If "A" is an atom, we might have

```
("A", "atom",  value)
```

For example: consider a program that processes queries based on Boolean combinations of keywords over a large database. One way to process a complex query is to build a parse tree representing the keyword expression to be applied to the database; each node applies a sub-transformation to a stream of database records produced by its inferiors—a node might *and* together two sorted streams, for example. All nodes run concurrently. A Linda program to accomplish this might involve workers executing a series of tasks that are in effect linked into a tree; the tuple that records each task includes "left", "right" and "parent" fields that act as pointers to other tasks [Nar88]. Graph structures in tuple space arise as well; for example, a simple shortest-path program [GCCC85] stores the graph to be examined one node per tuple. Each node-tuple has three fields: name of the node, an array of neighbor nodes (Linda supports variable-sized arrays in tuples), and an array of neighbor edge-lengths.

These linked structures have been fairly peripheral in our programming experiments to date. But there *is* one class of ordered structure that is central to many of the methods we've explored, namely streams of various kinds. There are two major varieties, which we call in-streams and read-streams. In both cases, the stream is an ordered sequence of elements to which arbitrarily-many processes may append. In the in-stream case, each one of arbitrarily-many processes may, at any time, remove the stream's head element. If many processes try to remove an element simultaneously, access to the stream is serialized arbitrarily at runtime. A process that tries to remove from an empty stream blocks until the stream becomes non-empty. In the read-stream case, arbitrarily-many processes read the stream simultaneously: each reading process reads the stream's first element, then its second element and so on. Reading processes block, again, at the end of the stream.

In- and read-streams are easy to build in Linda. In both cases, the stream itself consists of a numbered series of tuples:

```
("strm", 1, val1)
("strm", 2, val2)
...
```

The index of the last element is kept in a tail-tuple:

```
("strm", "tail", 14)
```

To append NewElt to "strm", processes use

```
in("strm", "tail", ? index);   /* consult tail pointer */
out("strm", "tail", index+1);
out("strm", index, NewElt);   /* add element */
```

An in-stream needs a head-tuple also, to store the index of the head value (i.e., the next value to be removed); to remove from the in-stream "strm", processes use

```
in("strm", "head", ? index);   /* consult head pointer */
out("strm", "head", index+1);
in("strm", index, ? Elt);       /* remove element */
```

(Note that, when the stream is empty, blocked processes will continue in the order in which they blocked. If the first process to block awaits the *jth* tuple, the next blocked process will be waiting for the $j + 1st$, and so on.)

A read-stream dispenses with the head-tuple. Each process reading a read-stream maintains its own local index; to read each element of the stream,

```
index = 1;
<loop> {
        rd("strm", index++, ? Elt);
        ...
    }
```

As a specialization, when an in-stream is consumed by only a single process, we can again dispense with the head-tuple, and allow the consumer to maintain a local index. Similarly, when only a single process appends to a stream we can dispense with the tail tuple, and the producer can maintain a local index.

In practice, various specializations of in- and read-streams seem to appear more often than the fully-general versions. The streams we've discussed so far are *multi-source, multi-sink* streams: many processes can add elements (multi-source) and remove or read-elements (multi-sink). Often, however, single-source or single-sink streams are sufficient.

Consider, for example, an in-stream with a single consumer and many producers. Such a stream occurs in one version of the prime-finding program we'll discuss: worker processes generate a stream, each of whose elements is a block of primes; a master process removes each element of the stream, filling in a primes-table as it goes.

Consider an in-stream with a single producer and many consumers. In a traveling salesman program[1], worker processes expand sub-trees within

---

[1] Written by Henri Bal of the Vrije Universiteit in Amsterdam.

the general search tree, but these tasks are to be performed not in random order but in a particular optimized sequence. A master process writes an in-stream of tasks; worker processes repeatedly remove and perform the head task. (This structure functions, in other words, as a distributed queue.)

Consider a read-stream with a single producer and many consumers. In an LU-decomposition program [BCGL88], each worker on each iteration reduces some collection of columns against a pivot value. A master process writes a stream of pivot values; each worker reads the stream.

3.3.1 Message passing and live data structures

We can write a message-passing program by sharply restricting the distributed data structures we use: in general, a message passing program makes use only of streams. The tightly-synchronized message passing protocols in CSP, occam and related languages represent an even more drastic restriction: programs in these languages use no distributed structures; they rely only (in effect) on isolated tuples.

It's simple, then, to write a message passing program. First, we use `eval` to create one process for each node in the logical network we intend to model. Often we know the structure of the network beforehand; the first thing the program does, then, is to create all the processes it requires. In some cases the shape of a logical network changes while a program executes; we can use `eval` to create new processes as the program runs. Having created the processes we need, we allow processes to communicate by writing and reading message streams.

Live data structure programs are also easy to write given the passive distributed structures we've discussed. Any distributed data structure has a live as well as a passive version. To get the live version, we simply use `eval` instead of `out` in creating tuples. For example: we've discussed streams of various kinds. Suppose we need a stream of processes instead of passive data objects. If we execute a series of statements of the form

```
eval("live stream", i, f(i)),
```

we create a group of processes in tuple space:

```
("live stream", 1, <computation of f(1)>)
("live stream", 2, <computation of f(2)>)
("live stream", 3, <computation of f(3)>)
...
```

If f is the function "factorial" (say), then this group of processes resolves into the following stream of passive tuples:

```
("live stream", 1, 1)
("live stream", 2, 2)
("live stream", 3, 6)
...
```

To write a live data structure program, then, we use eval to create one process for each element in our live structure. Each process executes a function whose value may be defined in terms of other elements in the live structure. We can use ordinary rd or in statements to refer to the elements of such a data structure. If rd or in tries to find a tuple that's still under active computation, it blocks until computation is complete. Thus a process that executes

```
rd("live stream", 1, ? x)
```

blocks until computation of f(1) is complete, whereupon it finds the tuple it's looking for and continues.

3.4 Exercises

1. Write a set of four routines to support the creation and manipulation of various stream types. create accepts one argument, describing the type of stream to be created. You should support three types: single-source multi-sink in-streams, multi-source single-sink in-stream and multi-source multi-sink in-streams. Thus create(SMS) creates a single-source, multi-sink in-stream. create yields a result (it can be an integer) that will henceforth be used as a stream identifier. Thus we can execute

```
NewStrm = create(SMS).
```

The put routine accepts two arguments: a stream id, and an integer to put on the stream. (We'll assume that all streams have integer elements only.) Thus,

```
put(NewStrm, j);
```

(Clearly, the fact that strm is an SMS-type stream must be recorded somewhere, so that put can do the right thing.) get accepts a stream identifier and returns an integer, if one is available:

```
elt = get(NewStrm);
```

(get may block, of course.) The close routine accepts a stream identifier and "closes" the designated stream. (You'll need to establish for yourself, based on your implementation, what it means to close a stream.)

Why can't read-streams be (conveniently) supported under this scheme?

Subsidiary question: assuming that you are storing open-stream information in a tuple, in what sense have you used C-Linda to implement a "distributed object?"—"object" in the sense of the word used by object-oriented languages? If C were itself an "object-oriented" language, would your implementation be simpler? (If you don't know what "object-oriented programming" is, (*a*) you must have spent the last five years in Western Samoa, (*b*) you can skip this subsidiary question, (*c*) if you want to find out what it is, start with *Simula Begin* by Birtwistle *et al.* [BDMN79].)

2. Build a distributed hash table in tuple space. The hash table will hold elements of some uniform, arbitrary type (pick whatever type you want). It will will have k buckets, each represented by (at least) one tuple. Buckets must capable of holding more than one element. You must insure that no part of the table is damaged in the event that many processes try to add elements simultaneously; you should also allow for as much concurrency as possible among users of the table. (It's clearly *not* satisfactory, for example, to allow only one process at a time to access the table.)

3. (*a*) Build a set of routines to create and manipulate vectors in tuple space.

```
NewVec = vector(n,k),
```

creates an n element vector with each element initialized to k. Assume that vectors have integer elements.

```
i = rdvec(NewVec, j)
```

returns the *jth* element of `NewVec`;

```
update(NewVec, j, i)
```

resets the *jth* element of `NewVec` to i. (*b*) Your implementation of *a* probably has the following behavior: if many processes try to update some element simultaneously, one will succeed immediately, another will wait for the first (will wait one update-time), a third will wait two update-times, and so on. Suppose that we want the following behavior instead: updating a vector element takes constant time. The cost does *not* rise as more processes attempt to update simultaneously. (As before, if many processes attempt to update simultaneously, the final state of the vector will reflect *one* of the update values; the rest will be lost.) Implement this new version. (*c*) Your implementation probably has the following behavior: the time it takes to execute `vector` increases linearly with n. Write a new version in which `vector`'s execution time increases with the log of n (so long as there are enough processors to allow all processes to execute simultaneously).

4. Implement Lisp-style lists in tuple space. Your implementation should support `cons`, `car` and `cdr`; atoms are stored in tuple space using whatever representation you want. `cons` yields a result that identifies a new

list (or cons cell); this identifier can serve as an argument to car, cdr or to cons itself. Note that it must be possible for *many* processes to "car-cdr" down the same list simultaneously.

5. Suppose you have a server process that executes function S for its clients: they invoke the server, sending an argument x; the server sends back the value of $S(x)$. (In the course of evaluating S it might perform any ordinary server activity. This server process might be a remote file system, or a print server, or a location server, or a date-and-time server or whatever. You don't need to worry about what the server actually does.)

(*a*) Write two routines, ServerS() and S(x). We create the server by executing

```
eval("Server S", ServerS());
```

Processes invoke the service it provides by executing

```
result = S(x);
```

Assume that S() yields an integer. Note that S() behaves like a *remote procedure call*: any process can invoke this routine; information is passed to some other process as a consequence, and a result is eventually returned to the invoking process (which remains blocked until the result arrives). In writing procedure S(), make sure that each invoking process gets the right answer back (*i.e.* gets the result that was intended for *it*). (A good way to do this involves a multi-source single-sink in-stream.)

(*b*) Write a routine LoadS() which returns the current "load average" on server S, defined as "the number of requests awaiting service from S."

(*c*) S might be a computational rather than a device-related service: it might (say) convert a printer file from one format to another, or remove noise from an image, or optimize a compiled program. If this kind of service is overloaded, we can start another identical server process (running, presumably, on some other processor). Write a routine that "pushes" a new instance of ServerS() on a "live stack" (a stack whose elements are processes) when the load average exceeds some figure, and pops the stack when the load average drops. Popping the stack will require that instances of ServerS() be aware of the existence of the stack; this routine should be rewritten in such a way that it terminates (or pops itself) when told to do so. A request for service should be handled by the first available server. Build "hysteresis" into your stack-management routine: it should resist overly-frequent pushes and pops.

(*d*) Again assuming a "computational" server, return to your original version of ServerS and modify it as follows: instead of receiving a request, acting on it and sending back the result, ServerS sends back a *process* that *computes* the requested result. Thus, clients send data values to the server; the server sends processes back. The interface routine, S(x), should *not* change.

Massive parallelism: 6. If you had a parallel machine with tens of thousands of processors and very cheap inter-processor communication, you might want to build active instead of passive data structures routinely. Write a new version of the vector routine discussed in question 3; the new routine creates "live vectors." The vector is realized as a tree of processes; vectors implement three operations: "update," "sum" and "sort."

    update(NewVec, j, i);

works as before.

    i = sum(NewVec)

causes NewVec to sum its elements and return the answer. The summing operation should require time that is logarithmic in the length of the vector.

    sort(NewVec)

causes NewVec to sort itself, again in logarithmic time.

Note that the structure you build will be wildly inefficient in current environments. (But it may be a harbinger of the future.)

□ 7. You can use distributed data structures to organize processes; to what extent are the same structures useful (in principle) for organizing people? Specifically: suppose you had a tuple space that could be accessed interpretively. You can write arbitrarily-many routines that put tuples into this space, or withdraw them; these routines never have to be linked together into a single program. Now, consider writing some routines that are invoked by users directly from an operating system command shell, and that deal with this tuple space. How would you write routines that (a) send another user mail, (b) post notices to a bulletin board on any topic (the topic is designated by a character string), and search the bulletin board for a notice on some topic; (c) allow many users to withdraw task assignments from a stream, add new assignments to the stream and monitor the current task backlog (i.e. the length of the stream)?

(Topics that relate to these questions are discussed in greater detail in chapter 9.)

☐ 8. Design and implement a distributed data structure that represents an (abstract) market. You can decide in advance which goods are for sale (this may be a market in, e.g., commodities A, B, C and D). The market implements two operations: buy one unit of something, and sell one unit, at the current prevailing price. In other words, it provides operations like buy(A) and sell(B). buy blocks if there are no sellers, sell if there are no buyers. Each commodity has some initial price. Thereafter, prices change dynamically and automatically, depending on supply and demand.

If a buyer shows up and finds exactly one seller waiting, the price doesn't change. If a seller shows up and finds one buyer, the price, again, doesn't change. If a buyer finds more than one seller waiting, the price drops; if a seller finds more than one buyer, it rises. (Use whatever function you want to adjust prices. If there is more than one buyer, for example, you might set the new price equal to

$$P + .01(L - 1)P,$$

where P is the old price and L is the length of the buyer's line.) Prices of each commodity are tracked in a distributed data structure. Your market must be able to support simultaneous invocations of buy and sell by many processes; action in one commodity should not exclude simultaneous action in other commodities. (This data structure is the basis for a further exercise in chapter 9.)

4 Performance Measurement and Debugging

4.1 Introduction

Before we set to work developing parallel programs, we need to consider two more basic questions of programming mechanics. *Debugging* parallel programs raises certain problems (centering on deadlock and non-determinism) that are new and different—although, as we discuss, the significance of these issues is rather modest in practical terms. *Performance analysis and tuning* is a crucial issue in parallel programming. The whole point is to write programs that run fast. Once an application is up and running, we must know how well we are doing, and how to do better. These two basic issues are closely related, in fact, in the sense that *performance debugging* is a crucial aspect of code development for parallelism. Once logical debugging is complete, we know that our code runs correctly. But a "performance bug" that makes a program run too slowly is, in one sense, every bit as significant as a "logic bug" that makes it compute incorrectly. A parallel program that doesn't run fast is, in most cases, approximately as useful as a parallel program that doesn't run at all.

4.2 Debugging

Debugging involves two issues—the *systems tools* you rely on to accomplish it, and the *logical questions* you expect to deal with. In the sequential world, symbolic debuggers are the main line of defense as far as tools go. The problems posed by sequential debugging are well known. In the following discussion, we consider debugging in the coordination language framework; then we move on to the special logical problems associated with parallel-program debugging.

4.2.1   Introduction: software tools for debugging in the coordination language framework

The debugging of parallel programs is often held up as a complex and arcane art, but (luckily) it isn't. The concepts of *coordination language* and *coordination framework* make it possible to deal with parallel debugging as an incremental extension to ordinary sequential debugging. A parallel program consists of some ordinary sequential programs bound together by a coordination framework. We *already know* how to debug the sequential programs—whatever approach you take to debugging sequential programs, and whatever tools you rely on, can in principle be carried over intact to the parallel environment. Parallel debugging reduces, accordingly, to the following question: how do we debug a coordination framework? So far as the tools are concerned, there is a high-tech and a low-tech approach.

In the high-tech approach we use a *coordination framework debugger* that relates to conventional sequential-language symbolic debuggers just as coordination languages relate to sequential languages. The coordination debugger shows you the *coordination state* of the program, and gives you access to sequential debuggers focussed on individual processes. Thus it organizes or "glues together" a collection of sequential debuggers in the same way that a coordination language glues together a collection of sequential processes.

In the low-tech approach, we improvise the coordination debugger, perhaps by creating multiple windows with a sequential debugger running in each. The low-tech approach sounds painful, and it is— particularly when you need to debug a large, diverse process ensemble. But it's important to note that there is a crucial relationship between programming methods on the one hand and debugging on the other. Master-worker programs have a fascinating characteristic: no matter how large they grow, they involve only *two kinds* of processes, and they run in exactly the same way (in logical terms) whether they are executed with one worker or with ten thousand. During the logical-debugging stage, we'll run such programs with a single master and a single worker (or two workers, to allow for any effects that appear only when there is concurrency among workers). The extent of the actual parallelism in such a program is (obviously) modest. The logistics of such an application are readily handled.

Simple master-worker programs (one master, many identical workers) give rise to more complicated variants. These may involve many specialized masters or several pools of workers. But the general principle still holds.

4.2.2 Tuplescope

The "high-tech" debugging/monitoring/visualization tool for Linda coordination frameworks is called Tuplescope. Tuplescope presents a "visualization" of tuple space (figure 4.1). One of Tuplescope's major functions is the coordination of debugging agents, just as Linda coordinates computation agents. Tuplescope initially offers the user a window on the contents of tuple space. This window is divided into panes representing disjoint spheres of activity. Operations acting on the tuples in one pane are of no interest to operations acting in another pane. Tuples and processes are represented iconically in the panes. As the computation unfolds, tuples appear and disappear, and processes flit from pane to pane as their foci change.

Each of the objects represented can be studied in greater detail by zooming in. A data tuple close-up reveals the structure of the tuple: its fields and their values. A process tuple becomes, upon closer scrutiny, a text window with Linda operations highlighted, while zooming closer still lays bare the process's code and environment to the prying eyes of a full-fledged debugger (a member of the dbx family, for example.)

Tuplescope is nice if you have it (or the equivalent for some other coordination language). If you don't, there are ways to make do without it. In either case, the logical problems of parallel debugging are the same.

4.2.3 Logical problems in parallel debugging

Viewers all over the county have noticed that, whenever the local TV news does a man-on-the-street interview spot, and the topic is parallel code development, responses show a striking consistency from Pasadena to Paramus. Everyone agrees that *non-determinacy* and *deadlock* are the lurking dangers. The man-on-the-street is right. These *are* problems that are peculiar to concurrent programs, problems that sequential

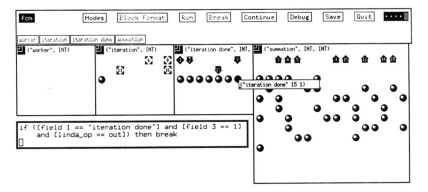

Figure 4.1
The Tuplescope visualizer.

Here, Tuplescope is focussed on a program whose tuple space has been partitioned into four panes. The panes are rectangles; each is labelled with a template summarizing the tuples whose activities are capture by the pane. (The nested square icon is a resize button—the pane ("summation", INT, INT) has been enlarged.) A data tuple is represented by a round icon. A live tuple (process) is represented by square-ish icon (labelled with the process's id): a fat arrow (upward pointing indicates the process's last Linda operation was an in; downward, an out) or a diamond (the process is blocked). Tuples can be "moused" to reveal the fields of a data tuple or the source for the last Linda operation executed by a live tuple. Debug scripts can be written to specify breakpoints based on a variety of conditions. The small window gives one such script. The figure displays tuple space at the moment this condition was triggered. The icon of the live tuple involved has been notched (Process 2) and the data tuple's icon has been flattened into a black disk. The data tuple icon has been moused to display its fields. A control panel, placed above the tuple space display, allows the user to set and change parameters altering the kind of information displayed, the amount, and the speed of update. It also allows the user to start and stop execution as well as activate debugging scripts.

debugging rarely faces. We're glad to report, however, that in most cases the dangers are actually quite modest.

Deadlock. It's not surprising that explicit concern with communication gives rise to a new class of bugs. The most fundamental is deadlock. Suppose we have a program with two components, processes A and B. If the program enters a state in which A is waiting for a tuple from B and B is waiting for a tuple from A, the program is deadlocked—no further progress will be made. Obviously more complex cases can (and do) occur. In the general case, an arbitrarily-long cycle will exist. The elements of the cycle are by turns *processes* and *resources* (in our case, *tuples*). Each process in the cycle owns the previous tuple (is the only process that can generate said tuple, in other words), and *wants* the next one.

A "feature" of deadlocks is that they cannot, in general, be distinguished from other cases in which a program is progressing slowly, or has died for some other reason (for example, some process has core dumped and the operating system hasn't told anyone). Hence, the program developer must know how to *detect* deadlock. We'll describe two approaches that have been used to detect deadlock in Linda programs. (Similar approaches are possible, of course, in other coordination languages.)

Some implementations look for deadlock at run time. The basis for such a method is a protocol that requires a check each time a process is blocked on a tuple request. If the process about to block is the last one *not* blocked, deadlock can be declared and we can all go home. All processes exit after writing a status message identifying themselves and the operation they are executing.

The details of this mechanism are not trivial; in fact, efficient implementations for some environments (*e.g.* local area networks) remains a research topic.

This mechanism suffers from the limitation that it detects only *total* deadlock. There are two common ways in which partial deadlock might occur. It may be that two processes are mutually deadlocked, effectively dropping out of the computation—and yet the computation is structured in such a way that it can still complete. Or some processes may be blocked on something other than a tuple space operation. If, in the simple example above, another process was blocked waiting, say, for input, it would never appear blocked on a tuple space operation, and thus the detection condition would not be satisfied. It would be possible to refine the detection scheme at the cost of complexity and reduced efficiency, but there's often a better way.

Detecting deadlock using Tuplescope is a simple matter: if all the process icons are in the blocked state, the program is deadlocked. (If *any* process icon remains blocked, there may be something wrong.)

Luckily, deadlock in parallel applications is a surprisingly infrequent problem. Mutual dependence is *not* a characteristic of most parallel computations. (It's more frequently an issue in distributed systems; we discuss the problem again, from this point of view, in chapter 9.) Typically, parallel applications use a sequence of tuples to represent the evolving computation state. Updates to the state are often accomplished *via* paired in and out operations. As long as the state variable is "created" (the tuple representing the initial state is outed), its existence is preserved over every update. Hence further updates and further read operations need never block indefinitely.

(Linda programmers do sometimes experience a problem that is vaguely related to deadlock—they write ins that almost, but don't quite, match their outs. The C-Linda linker flags in or rd statements for which no matching tuple will ever be generated. It remains the case, though, that generating a slightly wrong set of tuples—wrong in number or in content—can leave an in or rd statement hanging.)

Non-determinism. *Non-determinism* refers to those aspects of a program's behavior that can't be predicted from the source program. Linda's in operation, for example, is defined in such a way that *some* matching tuple is returned. We can't say which one. If *many* processes are blocked on similar in statements, and an out creates a tuple that will match any one of them, *some* blocked process will get the tuple and continue. But again, we can't predict which one.

This kind of "semantic non-determinism"—non-determinism that is an explicit part of a language definition—isn't an attribute of Linda *per se*, nor an attribute of parallel or coordination languages exclusively. It arises in circumstances where imposing a fixed order is unnatural, hence semantically inappropriate, and a burden on a language's users; hence too, an unnecessary restriction on the implementation. If many processes reach for a tuple *simultaneously*, the simplest and most natural thing to say is that "one of them gets it"—not that "the one in the red hat gets it," or "the one with lowest process id gets it," or whatever. Any such rule is likely to be arbitrary, and arbitrary (as opposed to logical) rules are best avoided. Not bothering the user with arbitrary rules also, of course, frees the implementation from enforcing arbitrary rules. The more freedom an implementation has, the more opportunity it has to do the easiest or the fastest thing at runtime. (The same may hold in sequential languages. The order in which arguments to a function are evaluated is generally left unspecified—to choose what is probably the most significant example.)

Another kind of non-determinism has to do not with the language definition (except in the most general sense), but with the execution model. When processes execute asynchronously, we can't say how each one's internal activities will relate to the others. On different runs, the relationships might be different. If processes P and Q each execute an out statement, sometime P's tuple may be generated first and other times Q's may be (unless there is some logical dependence between the operations).

In the context of result and agenda parallelism, non-determinism of all kinds tends to be a minor consideration, so far as debugging goes. In result-parallel codes, execution is governed by data-dependencies. A given process runs when and only when all the processes it depends upon have completed. Processes execute simultaneously exactly when they have *no* relationship at all. The one-worker debugging model for master-worker agenda parallelism sharply constrains the extent to which non-determinism can occur. This isn't a mere debugging trick, though—it points to a deeper issue. We can debug with a single worker because the program *behaves* as if it had only one worker, regardless of the number it actually *does* have. Worker processes have *no* direct inter-relationships. Any significant non-determinism will occur in the context of the master-worker relationship only.

Specialist parallelism can be more problematic. As we've seen, though, specialist parallelism is usually implemented using message passing. If we use ordered message streams, one kind of non-determinism is eliminated. Non-determinism still occurs with regard to the order in which processes are allowed to append messages to a multi-source stream, or remove them from a multi-sink stream. But most programs are insensitive to such non-determinism, which can of course be eliminated, if need be, by breaking one stream into many.

4.3 Performance

Once a parallel program has been written and debugged, it's incumbent upon the author to explore the code's performance. If it doesn't run faster as more processors are made available, at least up to a point, it's a failure.

The usual measures of parallel performance, and the ones we will concentrate on here, are speedup and efficiency. *Speedup* is the ratio of sequential run time to parallel run time. *Efficiency* is the ratio of speedup to number of processors.

Unfortunately, these apparently simple definitions conceal much complexity. For example, what do we mean by "sequential run time"? In measuring a parallel application's performance, we need to establish what we are gaining in *real* terms. A parallel program is ordinarily costlier than a conventional, sequential version of the same algorithm: creating and coordinating processes takes time. Running an *efficient* parallel program on many processors allows us to recoup the overhead and come out ahead in absolute terms. An *inefficient* parallel program, on the other hand, may demonstrate impressive *relative* speedup—it may run faster on many processors than on one—without ever amortizing the "overhead of parallelization" and achieving *absolute* speedup. (Readers should be alert to this point in assessing data on parallel programming experiments.)

Clearly, then, we need to benchmark our parallel programs against the "*comparable*" sequential version. Establishing what's "comparable," though, can be tricky. When a parallel application starts life as a sequential program, this sequential program may be the natural comparison point. In fact, most "real" parallel programs—programs that are developed for production use—*do* start life not as blank sheets of paper but as ordinary, sequential programs that run too slowly. But suppose that the most *natural* sequential starting point doesn't represent the most *efficient* sequential strategy? The best sequential algorithm may parallelize poorly; another approach, worse in the sequential case, may parallelize better. In these cases we are obliged, within reason, to compare the parallel program to a *different* sequential version that represents our best shot at good sequential performance.

Once we've decided what our two comparison programs will be, subtle questions remain. One of the most important and common has to do with differences in problem size. Solving the same size problem sequentially and in parallel can result in artifacts that reflect not the programming effort *per se*, but the memory hierarchy of the machine used in the comparison. We will run the sequential version on one processor of a parallel machine, and the parallel version on many processors of the *same* machine, to control for hardware as far as possible. But each sub-computation within a parallel program will generally be "smaller" than the sequential computation in its entirety. Because of the size difference, memory references in the parallel sub-computations may have a better chance of hitting in cache, yielding a performance benefit that is real but (in a sense) accidental. The aggregate memory of the parallel machine may (for distributed-memory machines, probably will) exceed the capacity of the node on which we execute the sequential version. This too can lead to faster memory access for the parallel code. Ought we to say, then, that a true comparison must compare the parallel program against a sequential version running on a *different* machine, one whose aggregate memory is the same size as the parallel machine's, or with a larger cache to compensate for the larger problem sizes, and so on? If so, we are writing a complex, burdensome and (ultimately) subjective list of requirements. It's more reasonable to acknowledge the fact that, in practice, it's almost impossible to avoid some element of "unfairness" in this kind of performance testing.

Scaling the problem to "fit" better for the sequential case represents another course of action, but this leads to its own set of problems. Obviously we can't *directly* compare a small sequential problem to a large parallel problem. But we can't restrict parallel testing to small problems only, because parallelism becomes more valuable as the problem size gets *larger*. The whole point, after all, is to run *large*, computationally *expen-*

sive problems well—not to be able to improve the performance of *small* problems that run adequately on conventional machines. Can we run a small sequential problem, and use a performance model to extrapolate its behavior to the larger problem sizes that we use in the parallel test runs? Yes, in principle. But different components of the computation may scale differently, and achieving a sufficiently accurate performance model to yield reliable figures will often prove a difficult exercise.

Our best bet, in sum, is to be reasonable, and to accept the inherent imprecision of the assignment. We will compare a parallel program with a "reasonable" sequential version. We'll run the sequential problem on one node of a parallel machine, and parallel versions of the same size problem on many nodes of the same machine. The next step is to study the performance figures, and attempt to understand them.

4.3.1   Modelling the behavior of parallel programs

As a first approximation, we can (or would like to) model performance by an expression of the form

$$\frac{a}{k} + b,$$

where a represents the amount of time taken by the *parallelized component* of the parallel program, b represents the time taken by the *serial component*, and k is the number of processors. We assume that the parallel and sequential programs are essentially the same algorithmically. Note, though, that a and b might *not* sum to the sequential time t_{Seq}. Both a and b may be larger than their counterparts in the sequential version. It's possible (in fact likely) that parallelization will add to both components—will add additional work that can be parallelized and additional work that cannot be. Ideally, we would like

$$a = t_{Seq},$$

$$b = 0.$$

But in practice, (parallelizable) overhead *will* be introduced when we write the parallel version, and there will also be some inherently serial parts of our algorithm (often including problem set up and take down, for example), and some inherently serial aspects of our coordination framework (for example, synchronization and certain communication costs).

Although we haven't explicitly indicated the dependence, both a and b can (and likely will) vary both with k and and with the size of the problem.

Assuming for the moment that a and b are essentially independent of k, consider what happens in two different cases: k is very large, and k is small.

First, suppose we are willing to buy performance by adding processors. We don't care about efficiency, so long as each new processor reduces run time. As k grows arbitrarily large, the ratio $\frac{t_{Seq}}{b}$ sets an upper limit on speedup.[1] To reduce this absolute limit on speedup, our only choice is to reduce b, the non-parallelizable part of the program.

Now, suppose that we are *not* blessed with an unlimited number of processors. If k is bounded by K (*i.e.* we are presented with a fixed number of processors), such that $\frac{a}{K} \gg b$, then b is no longer our major concern. If we consider efficiency (achieved speedup divided by the number of processors), we can derive a relation similar to the one for absolute speedup: efficiency is limited by $\frac{t_{Seq}}{a}$. Given a fixed number of processors, we can no longer tolerate ineffective use of a processor's computing time; we must minimize time wasted on overhead, by attempting to make $\frac{t_{Seq}}{a}$ as close to 1 as possible—in particular, by minimizing the (parallelizable) overheads we introduced when we turned our serial code into a parallel program. Of course we need the make sure that, in the process of doing so, we don't increase b significantly.

In other words: when we have an unlimited number of processors, efficiency (in principle) doesn't matter. We can neglect efficiency in two ways. We can leave some of our processors mostly idle; a mostly-idle processor can still contribute to absolute performance if it kicks in exactly when we need it (at a particularly compute-intensive juncture), and then goes back to sleep. Or, we can keep all of our processors busy full-time, but busy *ineffectively*—spending much of their time on overhead introduced during the process of parallelization. If processors waste most of

---

[1] This constraint is closely related to "Amdahl's Law":

$$speedup = \frac{1}{1 - f},$$

where f is the fraction of the code that can be parallelized. If none of the code can be parallelized, $f = 0$, and the maximum speedup is one—that is, no speedup. If all code is parallelizable, then $f = 1$ and potential speedup is, in the abstract, unlimited.

their time on overhead, we can still achieve good absolute performance: if performance is inadequate, we simply hire more processors. (This is the federal bureaucracy model of parallel computing). Performance in this setting is limited only by the unparallelizable portion of the program (by b). Given a *fixed* number of processors, however, we can no longer neglect efficiency. We must ensure that each processor wastes as little of its time on overhead as possible, by reducing a as much as we can.

In practical terms, our two cases reduce to the following possibilities. Either we have plenty of processors, in which case b may be a dominating factor; or processors are in short supply, in which case a may be a dominating factor (so long as b remains under control); or we may have some "intermediate" number of processors, in which we case we might concentrate on a *and* b.

If we build a parallel program and we aren't satisfied with its performance, we must decide which situation holds, and concentrate on the appropriate parameters. How do we go about this? First we need to accumulate some timing data; runtime for the sequential program, and runtime for the parallel program under a representative sampling of k's. Fitting the parallel runtime data to a curve of the form $a/k + b$ will tell us, first, whether the model even applies; second, the approximate values of a and b. We can use this information to decide which case holds. At maximum k, are there enough processors to make b the dominant term, are we still "processor-limited" (is $\frac{a}{n}$ the dominant term), or does some intermediate case hold?

To reduce b, we need to look for ways to reduce the non-parallelizable component of the overhead added by parallelization, *and* to parallelize more of the original code. I/O is often one important target for the second effort. In a sequential code, computation time may significantly outweigh I/O time—and so, naturally, little effort is wasted on making I/O efficient. In the parallel version, computation time may be reduced to a point at which I/O becomes a dominating cost. If so, we need to worry about making I/O efficient. Another good way to reduce b is to re-think the techniques that are used to synchronize computations. Inexperienced programmers often assert too much control—for example, they use queues or streams when bags might do. Bags (as we've discussed) aren't terribly important in sequential programming, but good parallel programmers use them whenever they can. Only one process at a time can append-to or remove-from a queue, but many processes can reach into a bag simultaneously. When we switch from data structures that force serialization to data structures that allow concurrency, we reduce b and improve performance.

If our performance is "processor-limited," we'll concentrate on reducing a (without increasing b). One useful technique for master-worker programs is to reduce the cost of task acquisition. Much of this cost is parallelizable—many workers can acquire tasks simultaneously—but the less time each worker spends at this activity, the better. In more general terms, we try to reduce the communication costs (typically as much a function of the *number* of communication events as the amount of material communicated) associated with each computation.

Increasing a can lead to better performance, in a special sense. When we increase the problem size, we obviously expect to increase total run time. But for many problems, a is close to t_{Seq}, and b grows more slowly than a as the problem size increases, thus increasing $\frac{t_{Seq}}{b}$ and with it, maximum possible speed up. (To restate this strategy: if you don't get good performance on a small problem, try a large problem.) For example: a matrix multiplication code may spend n^2 time setting up, but n^3 time computing, suggesting that maximum possible speedup will grow linearly with problem size[2]. Repeated timing trials for different values of n (for different problem sizes) can yield important information about how a and b depend on n, and thus to what degree altering problem size will alter performance.

Load balancing and work starvation. Although the $a/n + b$ expression is useful, it isn't guaranteed to be accurate. There are several reasons why it might fail. The most important is *load balancing*. A problem that decomposes into four tasks (or four specialists, or a four-element live data structure) won't achieve a speedup of greater than four regardless of what n is (regardless, that is, of how many processors we run it on). A more subtle but equally important effect occurs in cases where, for example, we have 36 tasks in a master-worker program. If the tasks are about equal in complexity, such a program is likely to finish no faster on 17 processors than on 12. Finishing time is determined by

---

[2]To put this yet another way: the f in Amdahl's law is often a function of the problem size—a fact that is frequently overlooked.

the most heavily-burdened worker. In the 12-processor case, the worker
with the greatest burden (and for that matter every other worker) does
three tasks. In the 17-processor case, the worker with the greatest burden *still* does 3 tasks. 15 of the others do only two tasks each—but
thereafter, they simply idle while the others finish up. We refer to this
kind of problem as *work starvation*, a phenomenon that occurs when a
good load balance is logically impossible.

Work starvation is the extreme case of a bad load balance, but it represents (after all) merely the end-point of a spectrum. Even where
a reasonable load balance *is* possible, achieving it may not be easy.
The research literature is full of *static scheduling* studies—recipes for
achieving a good distribution of the components of a parallel program
to the processors of a parallel machine. (We examine static scheduling in
greater detail in chapter 8.) Often, however, we can avoid load balancing
problems by using the master/worker approach. This strategy usually
achieves a good load balance without even trying: because workers grab
new tasks as needed, we reach an even load distribution dynamically.

There *are* cases in which dynamic task assignment isn't sufficient in itself.
Suppose our tasks vary greatly in complexity, and suppose that the last
task to be grabbed happens to be a complicated one. Every worker but
one may sit idle (all other tasks having been completed) while the final,
time-consuming task is processed. Such problems are best attacked by
switching from a task bag to an ordered task queue; we return to this
problem in chapter 6.

Granularity knobs. The most crucial issue in parallel performance
debugging is *granularity*. A coordination framework takes time to execute. The time invested in the coordination frame—in creating processes and moving information among them—must (in some sense) be
over-balanced by the time invested in computing. If it isn't, the overhead of coordination overwhelms the gain of parallelism, and we can't
get good performance. Concretely, a message-passing program won't
perform well if each specialist doesn't do "enough" computing between
message-exchange operations; a live data structure program won't perform well if each live data element does "too little" computing; a master-
worker program won't perform well if the task size is "too small." Ex-
ceeding the granularity bounds can lead to excessively large a's or b's
or both. If the overhead parallelizes, we may get an application with

good relative speedup, but poor absolute performance. If the overhead doesn't parallelize, our excessively fine-grained program may not speed up at all.

Little can be said about "correct granularity" in absolute terms, beyond the fact that, in every hardware environment, and for every coordination language, a "crossover point" exists beyond which an application is too fined-grained to perform well. In most cases, it's up to the programmer to discover this crossover point for himself.

Its rough attributes can be established on the basis of hardware. The cost of *communication* is usually the dominating factor in determining the crossover point. Adding a tuple to tuple space costs tens of microseconds on current-generation shared-memory parallel computers, hundreds of microseconds on distributed-memory parallel computers, tens of milliseconds on local area networks[3]. These differences reflect the obvious architectural distinctions: on networks, bits must be transported *via* a slow channel, on distributed-memory machines they go *via* a fairly fast channel, and on shared-memory machines, they barely get transported at all. (They are merely copied from one part of memory to another.) Exactly the same hierarchy of costs would hold if we were discussing message passing, or any other communication model, instead of Linda[4]. If the task size in any setting is *less than* the amount of time it takes to find the task and report the results, we are paying more in overhead than we're accomplishing in computation, and it's a good bet that our application cannot perform well.

Clearly we must avoid excessively-fine granularity. But granularity that's too large is also bad. It can lead to load-balance problems or (in the limit) to work starvation. Many smaller tasks lend themselves to a more-even distribution of work than fewer, larger tasks.

The best way to deal with the granularity issue is, we believe, by building

---

[3]The Linda Machine [ACGK88] is an exception. It's a distributed-memory machine on which Linda operations run as fast as they do on shared-memory architectures.

[4]It's important to note that the cost of executing Linda operations is dominated by the cost of transporting bits, not by the high-level aspects of the Linda model. It's often conjectured that Linda must be expensive to use because of associative matching; luckily, this conjecture is false. Almost all matching is handled not at runtime but at *compile time* and *link time*, by an optimizing compile-time system which, in effect, "partially evaluates" the runtime library with respect to a user's application [Car87, CG90].

applications with *granularity knobs*. It's desirable that granularity not be a *fixed* attribute of a program, but rather something that can easily be adjusted. We can use this tunability to achieve good performance on our initial host machine. We may well need to twiddle the dial again when we port to a different machine, particularly if the new environment has very different communication hardware. We make this technique concrete in the next chapter.

4.4   Exercises

1.   We've discussed the fact that tuple space is inherently non-deterministic: *some* process gets a matching tuple; a process gets *some* matching tuple. Non-deterministic isn't the same as *random*: if tuple space were *random*, *which* process or *which* tuple would be a random choice (without pattern over arbitrarily-many repetitions). (*a*) Suppose that tuple space operations *were* random in their behavior. Discuss the implications from a programmer's and also (in general terms) from an implementor's perspective. (*b*) Suppose, again, that tuple space is no longer non-deterministic; suppose now that tuple space operations are defined in a time-ordered way. A process that executes an in or a rd gets the *oldest* matching tuple (the one that was added to tuple space at the earliest point). If many processes are awaiting a tuple, the oldest blocked process (the one that started waiting at the earliest point) gets the tuple. Discuss the implications, again, from a programmer's and an implementor's perspective.

2. Read the "timing and tracing tools" section of the appendix (section 5). Now, do some measurements: how long do out, in and rd require on you implementation? How do their execution times vary with the size of the tuple? With the matching pattern specified by in or rd? With the number of active processes?

3. How long does it take to add a tuple to and remove it from a bag in your implementation? How long does it take to append elements to and remove them from in-streams (all three variants) and read streams? How long does it take to look elements up and add them to the hash table that was described in exercise 2 in the previous chapter?

☐ 4. How do granularity issues arise in human organizations? To what extent have higher communication rates altered the limits of acceptable granularity? To what extent does "finer task granularity" mean less worker autonomy?

5 Putting the Details Together

Finding all primes between 1 and n is a good example problem for two reasons. (1) It's not significant in itself, but there are significant problems that are similar; at the same time, primes-finding is simple enough to allow us to investigate the entire program in a series of cases. (2) The problem can be approached naturally under several of our conceptual classes. This gives us an opportunity to consider what's natural and what isn't, and how different sorts of solutions can be expressed.

5.1 Result parallelism and live data structures

One way to approach the problem is by using result parallelism. We can define the result as an n element vector; j's entry is 1 if j is prime, otherwise 0. It's easy to see how we can define entry j in terms of previous entries: j is prime if and only if there is no previous prime less than or equal to the square root of j that divides it.

To write a C-Linda program using this approach, we need to build a vector in tuple space; each element of the vector will be defined by the invocation of an `is_prime` function. The loop

```
for(i = 2; i < LIMIT; ++i) {
  eval("primes", i, is_prime(i));
}
```

creates such a vector. As discussed in section 3.2, each tuple-element of the vector is labelled with its index. We can now read the jth element of the vector by using

```
rd("primes", j, ? ok)
```

The program is almost complete. The `is_prime(SomeIndex)` function will involve reading each element of the distributed vector through the square root of i and, if the corresponding element is prime and divides i, returning zero[1]; thus

```
limit = sqrt((double) SomeIndex) + 1;

for (i = 2; i < limit; ++i) {
  rd("primes", i, ? ok);
  if (ok && (SomeIndex%i == 0)) return 0;
}
return 1;
```

The only remaining problem is producing output. Suppose the program is intended to count all primes from 1 through `LIMIT`. Easily done: we simply read the distributed vector and count i if i's entry is 1. The complete program is shown in figure 5.1.

5.2   Using abstraction to get an efficient version

This program is concise and elegant, and it was easy to develop. It derives parallelism from the fact that, once we know whether k is prime, we can determine the primality of all numbers from $k+1$ through k^2. But it's potentially highly inefficient: it creates large numbers of processes and requires relatively little work of each. We can use abstraction to produce a more efficient, agenda-parallel version. We reason as follows.

1. Instead of building a live vector in tuple space, we'll use a passive vector, and create worker processes. Each worker will choose some block of vector elements and fill in the entire block. "Determine all primes from 2001 through 4000" is a typical task.

---

[1] In practice it might be cheaper for the *ith* process to compute all primes less than root of i itself, instead of reading them via `rd`. But we're not interested in efficiency at this stage.

```
#define  LIMIT  1000

real_main()
{
    int      count = 0, i, is_prime(), ok;

    for(i = 2; i <= LIMIT; ++i) eval("primes", i, is_prime(i));

    for(i = 2; i <= LIMIT; ++i) {
        rd("primes", i, ? ok);
        if (ok) ++count;
    }
    printf("%d.\n", count);
}

is_prime(me)
        int                me;
{
    int                i, limit, ok;
    double             sqrt();

    limit = sqrt((double) me) + 1;

    for (i = 2; i < limit; ++i) {
        rd("primes", i, ? ok);
        if (ok && (me%i == 0)) return 0;
    }
    return 1;
}
```

Figure 5.1
Prime finder: Result parallelism.

Tasks should be assigned in order: the lowest block is assigned first, then the next-lowest block and so forth. If we've filled in the bottom block and the highest prime it contains is k, we can compute in parallel all blocks up to the block containing k^2.

How to assign tasks in order? We could build a distributed queue of task assignments, but there's an easier way. All tasks are identical in kind; they differ only in starting point. So we can use a single tuple as a next-task pointer, as we discuss in the matrix multiplication example in section 3.2. Idle workers withdraw the next-task tuple, increment it and then reinsert it, so the next idle worker will be assigned the next block of integers to examine. In outline, each worker will execute

```
while(1) {
  in("next task", ? start);
  out("next task", start + GRAIN);

  <find all primes from start to start + GRAIN>
}
```

GRAIN is the size of each block. The value of GRAIN, which is a programmer-defined constant over each run, determines the granularity or task size of the computation. GRAIN, in other words, is the granularity knob for this application. The actual code is more involved than this: workers check for the termination condition, and leave a marker value in the next-task tuple when they find it. (See the code in figures 5.2 and 5.3 for details.)

2. We've accomplished "abstraction" and we could stop here. But since the goal is to produce an efficient program, there's another obvious optimization. Instead of storing a distributed bit-vector with one entry for each number within the range to be searched, we could store a distributed *table* in which all primes are recorded. The ith entry of the table records the ith prime number. The table has many fewer entries than the bit vector, and is therefore cheaper both in space and in access time. (To read all primes up to the square root of j will require a number of accesses proportional not to $\sqrt{j}$ but to the number of primes through $\sqrt{j}$.)

A worker examining some arbitrary block of integers doesn't know *a priori* how many primes have been found so far, and therefore can't construct table entries for new primes without additional information. We could keep a primes count in tuple space, but it's also reasonable to allow a master process to construct the table.

We will therefore have workers send their newly-discovered batches of primes to the master process; the master process builds the table. Workers attach batches of primes to the end of an in-stream, which in turn is scanned by the master. Instead of numbering the stream using a sequence of integers, they can number stream elements using the starting integer of the interval they've just examined. Thus the stream takes the form

```
("result", start, FirstBatch);
("result", start+GRAIN, SecondBatch);
("result", start+(2*GRAIN,) ThirdBatch);
...
```

The master scans the stream by executing

```
for (num = first_num; num < LIMIT; num += GRAIN) {
  in("result", num, ? new_primes);

  <record the new batch for eventual output>;

  <construct the distributed primes table>;
}
```

This loop dismantles the stream in order, ining the first element and assigning it to the variable **new_primes**, then the second element and so on.

The master's job is now to record the results and to build the distributed primes table. The workers send prime numbers in batches; the master disassembles the batches and inserts each prime number into the distributed table. The table itself is a standard distributed array of the kind discussed previously. Each entry takes the following form

```
("primes", i, <ith prime>, <ith prime squared>)
```

We store the square of the *ith* prime along with the prime itself so that workers can simply read, rather than having to compute, each entry's square as they scan upwards through the table. For details, see figure 5.3.

3. Again, we could have stopped at this point, but a final optimization suggests itself. Workers repeatedly grab task assignments, then set off to find all primes within their assigned interval. To test for the primality of k, they divide k by all primes through the square root of k; to find these primes, they refer to the distributed *primes* table. But they could save repeated references to the distributed global table by building local copies. Global references (references to objects in tuple space) are more expensive than local references.

Whenever a worker reads the global *primes* table, it will accordingly copy the data it finds into a local version of the table. It now refers to the global table only when its local copy needs extending. This is an optimization similar in character to the *specialization* we described in section 2: it saves global references by creating multiple local structures. It isn't "full specialization", though, because it doesn't eliminate the global data structure, merely economizes global references.

Workers store their local tables in two arrays of longs called `primes` and `p2` (the latter holds the square of each prime). The notation `object: count` in a Linda operation means "the first `count` elements of the aggregate named `object`"; in an `in` or a `rd` statement, `? object: count` means that the size of the aggregate assigned to `object` should be returned in `count`.

5.3   Comments on the agenda version

This version of the program is substantially longer and more complicated than the original result-parallel version. On the other hand, it

performs well in several widely-different environments. On one processor of the shared-memory Sequent Symmetry, a sequential C program
requires about 459 seconds to find all primes in the range of 1 to three
million. Running with twelve workers and the master on thirteen Symmetry processors, the C-Linda program in figures 5.2 and 5.3 does the
same job in about 43 seconds, for a speedup of about ten and a half relative to the sequential version, giving an efficiency of about 82%. One
processor of an Intel Intel iPSC/2 requires about 421 seconds to run the
sequential C program; one master and sixty-three workers running on
all sixty-four nodes of our machine require just under 8 seconds, for a
speedup of about fifty two and a half and an efficiency of, again, roughly
82%. (The iPSC/2 is a so-called *hypercube*—a collection of processors
each equipped with local memory, arranged in such a way that each one
"sits" at one corner of an n dimensional binary cube. Communication
links run over the edges of the cube to each processor's $n-1$ neighbors.)

If we take the same program and increase the interval to be searched in
a task step by a factor of 10 (this requires a change to one line of code:
we define GRAIN to be 20,000), the same code becomes a very coarse-
grained program that can perform well on a local area network. Running
on eight Ethernet-connected IBM RT's under Unix, we get roughly a 5.6-
times speedup over sequential running time, for an efficiency of about
70%. Somewhat lower efficiencies on coarser-grained problems are still
very satisfactory on local area nets. Communication is far more expensive on a local area net than in a parallel computer, and for this reason
networks are problematic hosts for parallel programs. They are promising nonetheless because, under some circumstances, they can give us
something for nothing: many computing sites have compute-intensive
problems, lack parallel computers but have networks of occasionally
underused or (on some shifts) idle workstations. Converting wasted
workstation cycles into better performance on parallel programs is an
attractive possibility.

In comparing the agenda to the result-parallel version, it's important
to keep in mind that the more complicated and efficient program was
produced by applying a series of simple transformations to the elegant original. So long as a programmer understands the basic facts
in this domain—how to build live and passive distributed data structures, which operations are relatively expensive and which are cheap—

the transformation process is conceptually uncomplicated, and it can stop at any point.   In other words, programmers with the urge to polish and optimize (*i.e.*, virtually all expert programmers) have the same kind of opportunities in parallel as in conventional programming.

Note that for this problem, agenda parallelism is probably less natural than result parallelism. The point here is subtle but is nonetheless worth making. The most natural agenda-parallel program for primes finding would probably have been conceived as follows: apply T in parallel to all integers from 1 to *limit*, where T is simply "determine whether n is prime". If we understand these applications of T as completely independent, we have a program that will work, and is highly parallel. It's not an attractive solution, though, because it is blatantly wasteful: in determining whether j is prime, we can obviously make use of the fact that we know all previous primes through the square root of j.

The master-workers program we developed *on the basis of the result-parallel version* is more economical in approach, and we regard this version as a "made" rather than a "born" distributed data structure program.

5.4   Specialist parallelism

Primes finding had a natural result parallel solution, and we derived an agenda parallel solution. There's a natural specialist parallel solution as well.

The Sieve of Eratosthenes is a simple prime-finding algorithm in which we imagine passing a stream of integers through a series of sieves: a 2-sieve removes multiples of 2, a 3-sieve likewise, then a 5-sieve and so forth. An integer that has emerged successfully from the last sieve in the series is a new prime. It can be ensconced in its own sieve at the end of the line.

We can design a specialist parallel program based on this algorithm. We imagine the program as a pipeline that lengthens as it executes. Each pipe segment implements one sieve (specializes, that is, in a single prime). The first pipe segment inputs a stream of integers and passes the

```
real_main(argc, argv)
      int  argc;
      char  *argv[];
{
    int      eot, first_num, i, length, new_primes[GRAIN], np2;
    int      num, num_primes, num_workers, primes[MAX], p2[MAX];
    int      worker();

    num_workers  =  atoi(argv[1]);
    for  (i = 0; i < num_workers; ++i) eval("worker", worker());

    num_primes  =  init_primes(primes, p2);
    first_num  =  primes[num_primes-1]  +  2;
    out("next task", first_num);

    eot = 0;  /* Becomes 1 at "end of table"—i.e., table complete. * /
    for (num = first_num; num < LIMIT; num += GRAIN) {
      in("result", num,  ? new_primes:length);

        for  (i = 0;  i < length;  ++i, ++num_primes) {
          primes[num_primes]  =  new_primes[i];

          if (!eot) {
              np2  =  new_primes[i]*new_primes[i];
              if  (np2 > LIMIT) {
                 eot  =  1;
                 np2  =  -1;
              }
              out("primes", num_primes, new_primes[i], np2);
          }
        }
    }
    /* "? int" means "match any int; throw out the value" * /
    for  (i = 0;  i < num_workers;  ++i) in("worker",  ? int);

    printf("count: %d\n", num_primes);
}
```

Figure 5.2
Prime finder: Agenda parallelism (master).

```
worker()
{
    int        count, eot, i, limit, num, num_primes, ok, start;
    int        my_primes[GRAIN], primes[MAX], p2[MAX];

    num_primes = init_primes(primes, p2);

    eot = 0;
    while(1) {
        in("next task", ? num);
        if (num == -1) {
            out("next task", -1);
            return;
        }
        limit = num + GRAIN;
        out("next task", (limit > LIMIT) ? -1 : limit);
        if (limit > LIMIT) limit = LIMIT;

        start = num;
        for (count = 0; num < limit; num += 2) {
            while (!eot && num > p2[num_primes-1]) {
                rd("primes", num_primes, ?primes[num_primes], ?p2[num_primes]);
                if (p2[num_primes] < 0)
                    eot = 1;
                else
                    ++num_primes;
            }
            for (i = 1, ok = 1; i < num_primes; ++i) {
                if (!(num%primes[i])) {
                    ok = 0;
                    break;
                }
                if (num < p2[i]) break;
            }
            if (ok) {
                my_primes[count] = num;
                ++count;
            }
        }
        /* Send the control process any primes found. */
        out("result", start, my_primes:count);
    }
}
```

Figure 5.3
Prime finder: Agenda parallelism (worker).

residue (a stream of integers not divisible by 2) onto the next segment, which checks for multiples of 3 and so on. When the segment at the end of the pipeline finds a new prime, it extends the sieve by attaching a new segment to the end of the program.

One way to write this program is to start with a two-segment pipe. The first pipe segment generates a stream of integers; the last segment removes multiples of the last-known prime. When the last segment (the "sink") discovers a new greatest prime, it inserts a new pipe segment directly before itself in line. The newly inserted segment is given responsibility for sieving what had formerly been the greatest prime. The sink takes over responsibility for sieving the *new* greatest prime. Whenever a new prime is discovered, the process repeats.

First, how will integers be communicated between pipe segments? We can use a single-source, single-sink in-stream. Stream elements look like

```
("seg", <destination>, <stream index>, <integer>)
```

Here, `destination` means "next pipe segment"; we can identify a pipe segment by the prime it's responsible for. Thus a pipe segment that removes multiples of 3 expects a stream of the form

```
("seg", 3, <stream index>, <integer>)
```

How will we create new pipe segments? Clearly, the "sink" will use `eval`; when it creates a new segment, the sink detaches its own input stream and plugs this stream into the newly-created segment. Output from the newly-created segment becomes the sink's new input stream. The details are shown in figure 5.4.

The code in figure 5.4 produces as output merely a count of the primes discovered. It could easily have developed a table of primes, and printed the table. There's a more interesting possibility as well. Each segment of the pipe is created using `eval`; hence each segment turns into a passive tuple upon termination. Upon termination (which is signalled by sending a 0 through the pipe), we could have had each segment yield its prime. In other words, we could have had the program collapse upon termination into a data structure of the form

```
("source", 1, 2)
("pipe seg", 2, 3)
("pipe seg", 3, 5)
("pipe seg", 4, 7)
...
("sink", MaxIndex, MaxPrime)
```

We could then have walked over and printed out this table.

This solution allows less parallelism than the previous one. To see why, consider the result parallel algorithm: it allowed simultaneous checking of all primes between $k + 1$ and k^2 for each new prime k. Suppose there are p primes in this interval for some k. The previous algorithm allowed us to discover all p simultaneously, but in this version they are discovered one at a time, the first prime after k causing the pipe to be extended by one stage, then the next prime, and so on. Because of the pipeline, "one at a time" means a rapid succession of discoveries; but the discoveries still occur sequentially.

The specialist-parallel solution isn't quite as impractical as the result-parallel version, but it is impressively impractical nonetheless. Since both of these codes create fairly large numbers of processes, we tested them using a thread-based C-Linda implementation on the Encore Multimax[2]. Both programs needed about the same amount of time (1.4sec) to search the range from 1 to 1000 for primes on a "minimal" number of processors. (One represents the minimal number for the specialist code, but the result code requires a minimum of six processors.

---

[2]Linda's eval makes use of the underlying operating system in creating new processes. C-Linda's semantics don't require that any particular kind of process be created; either "heavy-weight" or "light-weight" processes will do. Light-weight processes, often called *threads*, are faster to create and more efficiently managed than standard heavy-weight processes, and Linda does *not* require the added services that heavy-weight processes provide. Hence threads are, in general, the implementation vehicle of choice for eval; but they aren't universally available. They are particularly hard to come by in current-generation distributed-memory environments. The running versions of both programs differ trivially from the ones shown in the figures.

```
real_main()
{
    eval("source",  source());
    eval("sink",  sink());
}

source()
{
    int     i,  out_index=0;

    for (i = 5; i < LIMIT; i += 2) out("seg",  3,  out_index++, i);
    out("seg",  3,  out_index,  0);
}

sink()
{
    int     in_index=0, num, pipe_seg(), prime=3, prime_count=2;

    while(1) {
        in("seg",  prime,  in_index++,  ? num);
        if (!num) break;
        if (num % prime) {
            ++prime_count;
            if (num*num < LIMIT) {
                eval("pipe seg",  pipe_seg(prime,  num,  in_index));
                prime = num;
                in_index = 0;
            }
        }
    }
    printf("count:  %d.\n",  prime_count);
}

pipe_seg(prime,  next,  in_index)
{
    int     num,  out_index=0;

    while(1) {
        in("seg",  prime,  in_index++,  ? num);
        if (!num) break;
        if (num % prime) out("seg",  next,  out_index++, num);
    }
    out("seg",  next,  out_index,  num);
}
```

Figure 5.4
Prime finder: Specialist parallelism.

On fewer than six processors, our thread system is unable to handle the
blizzard of new processes.) The specialist code showed good relative
speedup through 4 processors (.35sec). The result code didn't speed up
at all.

So it looks like the specialist code did well—right? Wrong. The sequential code needed only .03sec to examine the first thousand integers; in
other words, the specialist code on four processors ran over ten times
slower then the sequential code. This result is an instructive demonstration of the phenomenon we discussed in the previous chapter—the
fact that a program can show good *relative* speedup—may run faster on
many processors than on one—without ever amortizing the "overhead
of parallelization" and achieving *absolute* speedup.

We expect technology to move in a direction that makes finer-grained
programming styles more efficient. This is a welcome direction for several reasons. Fine-grained solutions are often simpler and more elegant than coarser-grained approaches, as we've discussed; larger parallel machines, with thousands of nodes and more, will in some cases
require finer-grained programs if they are to keep all their processors
busy. But the coarser-grained techniques are virtually guaranteed to
remain significant as well. For one thing, they will be important when
parallel applications run on loosely-coupled nodes over local- or wide-
area-networks. (Whiteside and Leichter have shown that a Linda system
running on fourteen VAXes over a local area network can, in one significant case at least, beat a Cray [WL88]. This Cray-beating Linda
application is in production use at Sandia National Laboratory in Liv-
ermore.) Coarser-grained techniques will continue to be important on
"conventional" parallel computers as well, so long as programmers are
required or inclined to find maximally-efficient versions of their programs.

For this problem, our specialist-parallel approach is clearly impractical.
Those are the breaks. But readers should keep in mind that exactly
the same program structure *could* be practical if each process had more
computing to do. In some related problem areas this would be the case.
Furthermore the dynamic, fine-grained character of this program makes
it an interesting but not altogether typical example of the message-
passing *genre*. A static, coarse-grained message-passing program (of the
sort we described in the context of the n-body problem, for example)

would be programmed using many of the same techniques, but would be far more efficient.

5.5 Conclusions

In the primes example, one approach is the obvious practical choice. But it's certainly *not* true that, having canvassed the field, we've picked the winner and identified the losers; that's not the point at all. The performance figures quoted above depend on the Linda system and the parallel machine we used. Most important, they depend on the character of the primes problem. Agenda-parallel algorithms programmed under the master-worker model are often but not always the best stopping point; all three methods can be important in developing a good program. Discovering a workable solution may require some work and diligence on the programmer's part, but no magic and nothing different in kind from the sketch-and-refine effort that's typical of all serious programming. All that's required is that the programmer understand the basic methods at his disposal, and have a programming language that allows him to say what he wants.

5.6 Exercises

1. The primes-finder will run faster if it uses "striking out" instead of division—instead of dividing by k, it steps through an array and marks as non-prime every kth element. Re-implement the agenda-parallel program using this approach.

2. In the agenda-parallel primes-finder, what limit does the value of GRAIN impose on achievable speedup?

3. We transformed the result parallel primes-finder into an efficient program by abstraction to agenda parallelism. One aspect of the result version's inefficiency was its too-fine granularity; but it's possible to build a coarser-grained *result* parallel version of this code too. Implement a variable-granularity result-parallel version.

4. In the specialist-parallel primes-finder, the pipe segment responsible

for sieving out multiples of 3 is heavily overloaded. We expect that large backlogs of candidates will await attention from this process. Design a new version of the specialist-parallel program in which pipe segments can be replicated—in particular, multiple copies of the 3-sieve run simultaneously at the head of the pipeline.

□ 5. At the start of the industrial revolution, the British cotton industry faced the same kind of bottleneck as the specialist-parallel primes finder: "It took three or four spinners to supply one weaver with material by the traditional method, and where the fly-shuttle speeded up the weavers' operations the shortage of yarn became acute [Dea69, p. 86]." The answer was (in essence) exactly what we suggested in question 4; the solution hinged on one of the most famous gadgets in engineering history. How was the problem solved? What was the gadget?

6 Databases: Starting with Agenda

We turn now to "real problems." Our intention is to investigate three programs in detail: a natural agenda-parallel, a natural result-parallel and finally a natural specialist-parallel example. The final *solutions* won't fall into these three categories, of course; the starting points will. In each case, we'll arrive at an efficient agenda-parallel solution in the end. But our travels from the starting point to the goal will follow three very different routes. (Chapter 9, by the way, presents a program which does *not* get transformed into an agenda parallel version.)

Our intention in each chapter is to describe a problem, explain how a parallel solution was developed, and consider the performance of the solution. In concluding sections and in the exercises, we discuss the application of related techniques to other problems. A real problem isn't necessarily a complicated one; the problem we discuss in this chapter is quite simple. The problems in succeeding chapters are admittedly somewhat more complicated, but easily encompassed nonetheless in a single chapter each. Parallelism as a *real problem-solving technique* isn't restricted to enormous codes or complex problems. And great progress can be made through the use of simple techniques, so long as the techniques are chosen well and applied carefully.

6.1 Big issues

(We begin this and each of the following two chapters by distinguishing the *major themes* common to all three from the *special considerations* that distinguish each problem.)

Main themes:

> *Load balance* is crucial to good performance. The master-worker structure is a strong basis for building parallel applications with good load-balance characteristics.

Special considerations:

> *Watermark techniques* can meter the flow of data from a large database to a parallel application. *Large variance in task size* calls for special handling in the interests of good load balance. An ordered task stream is one possible approach.
>
> *Hardware and operating-system support for parallel I/O would be nice,* but can't be assumed. We need to develop techniques that don't rely on it; but programmers should also know how to take advantage of it.

6.2   Problem: database search with a complex search criterion

Suppose users need to search or examine every element in a database, and a fair amount of computing is required to examine each element. The example we will discuss involves DNA sequences. When a new sequence is discovered, geneticists may need to find out which previously-unravelled sequences the new one resembles. To do so, they may need to examine a large database of existing sequences. Obviously, the time necessary to examine the database increases with the size of the database. As the database grows, examination time may go from seconds to minutes to hours, crossing a series of cost and inconvenience thresholds along the way.

Comparing two long sequences is time-consuming, and such comparisons can be parallelized. However, geneticists usually require not a single comparison, but an extensive series of comparisons in which the target is compared against all or a major portion of a large database. It's clear, then, that we should consider parallelizing not the sequence-to-sequence comparison, but the database search—our program can perform many *sequential* comparisons *simultaneously*. This is the approach we'll discuss here. Parallelizing the comparison of two sequences (and forgetting about the rest of the database) is an interesting approach also; we discuss it in the next chapter.

The DNA database problem closely resembles others in many domains. There are lots of reasons to walk through every element of a large database, performing computations along the way. Consider one of the paradigm problems of commercial data processing, preparing bills. Phone companies, for example, devote enormous amounts of computing power (typically in the form of large mainframes) to a perpetual slog through swamps of customer records. Bills may go out to each customer monthly, but the bill-preparation process may go on full-time, around the clock. (Such problems can be dominated by sequential I/O costs; but I/O as well as computation can be parallelized.) There are many related examples in commercial data processing. Many types of library searches fall into this category too—you might have a database of chemical abstracts, or images, or news stories, and you need to apply some comparison-and-retrieval function to each one. The DNA-database problem itself is increasingly significant, as the Human Genome project adds enormously to the volume of our genetic knowledge. The larger point, of course, has nothing to do with this particular problem, nor even with the large class of related problems (like bill preparation); we are treating database search merely as one example of natural agenda parallelism. But the database problem does have wide applicability.

6.3   The problem description, and the agenda approach

You are given a function *compare*; it accepts two character strings representing DNA sequences as arguments; it yields a positive integer result. The closer the biological resemblance between sequences s and t, the greater the result yielded by *compare(s,t)*. Given a target sequence T, you must compute *compare(s, T)* for every sequence s in a database of sequences. You return an ordered list of all sequences whose closeness to T is greater than some cutoff value (or the single closest match, as the case may be).

Recall that we posed essentially this problem earlier, in discussing agenda parallelism and its manifestation in master-worker programs:

> Suppose we have a database of employee records, and we need to identify the employee with (say) the lowest ratio of salary to dependents. Given a record Q, the function

$r(Q)$ computes this ratio. The agenda is simple: "apply function r to all records in the database; return the identity of the record for which r is minimum." We can structure this application as a master-worker program in a natural way: the master fills a bag with data objects, each representing one employee record. Each worker repeatedly withdraws a record from the bag, computes r and sends the result back to the master. The master keeps track of the minimum-so-far, and when all tasks are complete, reports the answer.

This is exactly the kind of solution we'll describe here.

6.4   The sequential starting point

For the moment, let's forget about parallelism. How do we solve this kind of problem sequentially? The basic control structure is a loop in which the "important" computation is independent from one iteration to the next. But there is some auxiliary set up (*e.g.* setting the value of the iteration variable) and clean up (*e.g.* collating results from the computation) that may involve inter-iteration dependencies: swinging through the loop for the nth time may require that we have already swung through it for the $n - 1st$ time.

In this particular case, we iterate over all sequences in the database. The set-up extracts one sequence from a data base, the computation assesses its similarity to the target and the clean-up updates the "best" result if the current result exceeds the best so far:

```
while (TRUE) {
  done = get_next_seq(seq_info);
  if (done) break;
  result = compare(target_info, seq_info);
  update_best(result);
}

output_best();
```

We assume appropriate definitions for the data structures and functions. That we *can be* oblivious to this information, and in particular to the exact details of the comparison function, is an important feature of this approach. The parallel code that we will develop treats the comparison function as a "black box." This means not only that we can develop the coordination framework without worrying about the computations to be embedded within it; it also makes it possible to offer the user a *choice* of computations. A number of different sequence-comparison functions are available. The user might be invited to plug any function he likes into our framework. For that matter, virtually any kind of exhaustive database search can be handled using the general approach we're describing.

Agenda parallelism is a natural for this domain: our focus is drawn to the "how," not the "who" (specialists) or the "what" (result). We conceive of this problem in terms of a simple agenda of tasks (look at every record in the database) which many workers can clearly attack simultaneously. As we'll see, the natural solution is also an efficient one. It requires some tuning and optimization, but no basic transformation.

As usual, though, real problems are a bit more complicated than ideal ones. Our sequential code fragment presents two possible barriers to a simultaneous attack by identical workers. We must examine the following question: how are the ith and $i + 1st$ iterations of `get_next_seq()` and `update_result()` related? We can do lots of comparisons simultaneously, but we can't necessarily do lots of `get`s and `update`s simultaneously. (In principle, we might also worry about simultaneous invocations of `compare()` itself. But in this and many related domains, it is in fact okay to perform many simultaneous comparisons.)

`get_next_seq(seq_info)` seems in fact, for our application, to be inherently sequential. If we have one file on a conventional file-system device, we can't do many *reads* simultaneously. We must do them one at a time. We'll accept this limitation for now (we will discuss ways of relaxing it later on). Thus, our agenda contains one task that should be broken off and attacked sequentially by a single worker. One process in our ensemble will be devoted to reading the database record-by-record, making its contents available to the other workers.

`update_result()` finds the largest result (or the n largest) in the set of all results. There is no reason to believe that the outcome will be sensi-

tive to the order in which the results are processed. For the problem at
hand, there is in fact no such sensitivity. It is conceivable, however, that
the update process might be asked to log all results in a file. While the
actual order in which results appear in the file could be unimportant,
the fact that they are all being written to the same file suggests (on analogy with data input) that invocations of `update_result()` be executed
serially, and for the time being we will work under this assumption.
Thus, we will commission another process to perform result-updating
sequentially, result-by-result. Later on we will be a bit more careful
to distinguish between the "real" work of this routine (arriving at an
overall best value) and its possible role in generating output.

6.5   A first parallel version

Armed with this understanding of the dependencies between iterations
of the basic loop, we can sketch our first parallel version. We will have
sequential input process (a master), a swarm of comparison processes
(workers), and a sequential output process (standing on its own or, con-
ceivably, subsumed by the master process). We can now expand our
sequential code into skeletons for three kinds of processes:

Input
```
while (get_new_seq(seq_info)) {
  generate_task(seq_info);
}
```

Comparison
```
while (get_new_task(task_info)) {
  generate_result(compare(target_info, task_info);
}
```

Output
```
while (get_result(result_info)) {
  update_result(result_info))
}
```

The reader is entitled to feel a little misled—aren't we adding a dash of
specialist-parallelism to our agenda approach? Yes. It's reasonable to

describe the *input* and the *output* processes precisely as specialists. This kind of heterogeneity is crucial to real programming: the point is to find a good solution, not to impose a dogmatic framework. It's important to note, though, that the bulk of the computation will be handled by the multiple workers attacking the *comparison* tasks. What we've sketched is only a small variation on the standard master-worker coordination framework.

In fact, returning to the issue of input and output, the output task is trivial for our application. There is no good reason to create two separate processes for input and output; it's more reasonable to have the master do both.

With this modification, we can now present the code (figures 6.1 and 6.2). Several details will help in understanding it. All records in the database have a fixed-size header followed by the (variable length) sequence; **dbe** holds the entire record, while **dbs** is an offset that points to the sequence proper. The header includes information that identifies the sequence; this information is reduced to some unique integer label by **get_db_id()**. The actual similarity assessment is accomplished by the routine **similarity()**. Don't worry about its seemingly strange collection of arguments for now. This routine is recycled for further use in the next chapter, and the meaning of its arguments will become clear later on.

This code uses the simple but important "poison pill" technique to shut itself down. When the master has gathered the results it needs, it dumps a task tuple with a special value into tuple space. A worker ingesting this death tuple spits it back out into tuple space, then quietly falls on its sword.

> *About the program examples in this and in subsequent chapters:* the code given in the figures is derived from, but not identical to, working code. In order to clarify the presentation (and in particular to fit each module onto a single page), we've omitted **int** declarations, **void** function declarations, **struct** definitions and **#define** constants. We've also omitted various sanity checks for error conditions that, while necessary for robust code, are logically irrelevant. Finally, in times of acute need, we have resorted to replacing

statement conditionals by expression conditionals. Thus, instead of

```
if (p) then s1 else s2,
```

we have

```
(p) ? e1 : e2.
```

e1 and e2 are ordinarily the same as s1 and s2. This transformation typically allows us to collapse four lines into one, but the effect may be jarring to readers unfamiliar with C. They can find an explanation of expression conditionals (should they feel the need for one) in any good C text.

The transformation from a sequential to a parallel program has been easy (so far)—almost trivial. But this simple example illustrates many aspects of the typical candidate for agenda parallelism. Often, problems in this class are (or can be viewed as) iterative, with each iteration being largely independent of the others. Where there are dependencies, they often occur in the parcelling-out of input data or the collation of the results, not in the computation that transforms a bit of data from input to result. When starting from a sequential code that exploits this structure, it's often extremely simple to convert the sequential control loop into parallel control loops, as we've just done[1].

6.6   Second version: Adding "Flow Control"

So far, we've kept the problem specification simple. It's now time to confront issues that will occur when we try to solve real problems using

---

[1] In fact, the transformation is so simple that in many cases it can be performed automatically by a parallelizing compiler, or expressed via primitive syntactic constructs like "execute all iterations of this loop simultaneously"—a PARDO, DOALL, forall or some other construct as the case may be. But these alternatives grow far less effective when the going gets a bit tougher than this, as it will—when the required coordination framework isn't quite so simple. General-purpose languages like C-Linda can handle the simple *and* the complicated cases. And as we've seen, the easy cases are easily handled in C-Linda.

```
char dbe[MAX + HEADER], target[MAX];
char *dbs = dbe+HEADER;

real_main(argc, argv)
      char          **argv;
{
   t_length = get_target(argv[1], target);
   open_db(argv[2]);
   num_workers = atoi(argv[3]);

   /* Set up. */
   for (i = 0; i < num_workers; ++i) eval("worker", compare());
   out("target", target:t_length);

   /* Loop putting sequences into tuples. */
   tasks = 0;
   while(d_length = get_seq(dbe)) {
      out("task", get_db_id(dbe), dbs:d_length);
      ++tasks;
   }
   close_db();

   /* Get results. */
   real_max = 0;
   while (tasks—) {
      in("result", ? db_id, ? max);
      if (real_max < max) {
         real_max = max;
         real_max_id = db_id;
      }
   }
   /* Poison tasks. */
   for (i = 0; i < num_workers; ++i) out("task", 0, "":0);

   print_max(db_id, real_max);
}
```

Figure 6.1
Database search: First version (master).

```
char dbe[MAX + HEADER], target[MAX];
char *dbs = dbe+HEADER;

/* Work space for a vertical slice of the similarity matrix. */
ENTRY_TYPE col_0[MAX+2], col_1[MAX+2], *cols[2]={col_0,col_1};

compare()
{
    SIDE_TYPE            left_side, top_side;

    rd("target", ? target:t_length);
    left_side.seg_start = target;
    left_side.seg_end = target + t_length;

    top_side.seg_start = dbs;

    while (1) {
        in("task", ? db_id, ? dbs:d_length);

        if (!d_length) break;

        /* Zero out column buffers. */
        for (i=0; i <= t_length+1; ++i) cols[0][i]=cols[1][i]=ZERO_ENTRY;

        top_side.seg_end = dbs + d_length;
        max = 0;
        similarity(&top_side, &left_side, cols, 0, &max);
        out("result", db_id, max);
    }
    out("worker done");
}
```

Figure 6.2
Database search: First version (worker).

this program. In the process, we'll expose some deficiencies in our first-cut solution.

In reality, we will want to search large databases. (The genetics databases of interest are currently tens of megabytes large; in the future they will contain hundreds, potentially thousands of megabytes of data.) Furthermore, the databases to be searched contain records that vary enormously in size. (Genetics databases currently contain sequences ranging in size from tens to ten-thousands of bases.) Both of these facts present challenges to our parallel code. We'll attack the large-database problem here and the large-variance problem in the following section.

Clearly, we can't assume that a large database will fit *in toto* into main memory. But our current program rests implicitly on exactly this assumption. There is nothing to prevent the input process from running so far ahead of the comparison workers that it dumps the entire database into tuple space before the workers have even made a dent in the accumulating pile of sequences.

This problem didn't arise in our sequential version. The sequential code required merely that the target and one database sequence be inspected (hence be present in memory) at any given time. In the abstract, we could do something analogous in the parallel version. We could allow exactly one sequence per worker into tuple space at any given time. But this scheme forces a greater degree of synchronization between the input process and the workers. There is no *a priori* reason why the input process should have any idea what the comparison workers are up to; keeping it informed complicates the coordination framework and adds overhead.

> *Pop Quiz:* Sketch a solution that works in this way: at any given time, tuple space holds at most n sequences, where n is the number of workers.

There are other ways of achieving the same end, but they are also problematic. We could have every worker read sequences directly for itself as needed. This will only be acceptable, however, if we have parallel I/O capabilities on our machine: we must have the hardware and the software to allow many simultaneous accesses to a file. Some parallel-programming environments provide this kind of support, but most don't (yet). It isn't safe to assume that we have it.

The case for an oblivious input process is strong, but the problem remains: this process could potentially flood tuple space with sequence data. Given that it's harder to force vendors to supply adequate parallel file access capability than it is to modify our input/worker synchronization, we choose the latter strategy. We use a "high watermark/low watermark" approach to control the amount of sequence data in tuple space. (See for example Comer [Com84] for a discussion of watermark control in operating systems.) The idea is to maintain the number of sequences between an upper and a lower limit (the high and low watermarks). The upper limit ensures that we don't flood tuple space, the lower limit that we don't parch workers (that workers will be guaranteed to find a sequence tuple whenever they look for one)[2].

To carry this scheme out, we need some extra synchronization. Whenever a worker completes a comparison, it dumps a **done** tuple into tuple space. To start out, the input process **outs** h sequences, where h is the high-water mark. It then collects d **done** tuples, where d is the difference between the high and low watermarks; whereupon it resumes pumping sequences **out**. Both limits are fuzzy. The input process's count of outstanding sequences is approximate—it's always $\geq$ the "true" number. In practice this presents no difficulties: watermark schemes, this one included, rarely require that upper or lower bounds be hit precisely.

The code for the watermark version is given in figure 6.3. Only the master required modification, and so we give its code only. The workers are the same as they were in the previous version.

> *Pop Quiz:* Sketch a program in which the input process always knows the *exact* number of outstanding sequences.

---

[2]Strictly speaking, we should be concentrating not on the number of sequences but on the total *length* of the sequences in tuple space. We don't do this simply because in practice, we don't need the extra "accuracy" of the latter approach.

```
char dbe[MAX + HEADER], target[MAX];
char *dbs = dbe+HEADER;

real_main(argc, argv)
        char            **argv;
{
    t_length = get_target(argv[1], target);
    open_db(argv[2]);
    num_workers = atoi(argv[3]);
    lower_limit = atoi(argv[4]);
    upper_limit = atoi(argv[5]);

    /* Set up. */
    for (i = 0; i < num_workers; ++i) eval("worker", compare());
    out("target", target:t_length);

    /* Loop putting sequences into tuples. */
    real_max = 0;
    tasks = 0;
    while(d_length = get_seq(dbe)) {
        out("task", get_db_id(dbe), dbs:d_length);
        if (++tasks > upper_limit) /* Too many tasks, get some results. */
            do {
                in("result", ? db_id, ? max);
                if (real_max < max) {
                    real_max = max;
                    real_max_id = db_id;
                }
            } while (—tasks > lower_limit);
    }
    close_db();

    /* Get remaining results. */
    while (tasks—) {
        in("result", ? db_id, ? max);
        if (real_max < max) {
            real_max = max;
            real_max_id = db_id;
        }
    }
    /* Poison tasks. */
    for (i = 0; i < num_workers; ++i) out("task", 0, "":0);

    print_max(db_id, real_max);
}
```

Figure 6.3
The modified master, with watermarking.

6.7 Third Parallel Version: Ordering Sequences to Improve Load Balancing

Having addressed the issue of fitting a large database into a small space (an issue of interest for *all* database applications), let's tackle the implications of wide variance in sequence length. The first question is "what's the problem?" It comes down to *load balance*. Suppose we have lots of short sequences and one very long one. Suppose that the last task chosen by the last worker involves the very long one. While every other worker sits idly (all other tasks having been completed), this one unfortunate worker hacks away at his final, extra-long task.

For example: suppose we have a database consisting, in aggregate, of 10^6 bases, that the longest single sequence is 10^4 bases and the rest are of roughly equal length. (Say they're 100 bases each.) Now assume that we have deployed 20 comparison workers to search this database. If the long sequence is picked up near the end of the computation, we will have one comparison worker scanning $\sim 60,000$ bases (i.e. an extra ten thousand) while the rest scan $\sim 50,000$ bases each. Assuming that each worker's compute time is proportional to the total number of database bases it scans, we see that we will achieve a speedup of ~ 17, significantly less than the ideal 20.

Pop Quiz: Why? Justify the claimed 17-times speedup.

If, on the other hand, the long sequence is picked up early, the natural load balancing properties of our program will result in all workers doing about the same amount of work, and together achieving a speedup close to the ideal.

This last observation suggests an obvious attack on the problem. As part of the work done in preparing the database, order it longest sequence first. Then, instead of a bag of sequences, maintain an ordered list of sequences in a one-source multiple-sink stream. The comparison workers process this stream in order, ensuring that the longest sequences are done first, not last.

Once again, we solve a problem by introducing additional synchronization. This time it isn't between the input and comparison processes (recall there is no interprocess synchronization for the writer of a one-source/many-sink stream), but between the comparison processes themselves, in the form of the tuple used to index the stream. Here, synchronization is added to address an efficiency concern—but adding synchronization to solve an efficiency problem is extremely non-intuitive. We've balanced the load across the workers, but at the cost of introducing a potential bottleneck. Each worker needs to access the index tuple to acquire a sequence (a task). Suppose that the time required to do a task is too short to allow all other workers to access the index tuple. In this case, when the first worker (now done with the last task) reaches for the index tuple again, it's likely that at least one other worker will also want to claim the index tuple. The more workers in the field, the more time will be spent contending for the index tuple.

For example: suppose that updating the index tuple takes 1 unit of time and *every* comparison takes the same amount of time, say 100 units. Now if we start 10 workers at once, the time at which they actually start doing comparisons will be staggered: at time 0, one worker updates the index tuple (it will begin computing at time 1), some other worker grabs the index tuple at time 1 (and start computing at time 2) and so on. The last worker gets his shot at the index tuple at time 9 and starts computing at time 10. As of time step 10 all workers are busy, and they will remain so until time step 101. At this point the first worker will have finished its first task. It proceeds to grab the index tuple in order to learn the identity of its next sequence. The process repeats, with the result that all workers (except for a brief start-up and shut-down phase) are kept busy with only a 1% task-assignment overhead per task.

If we have 200 workers, however, we have a problem. The first round of work will not have been played out until time 200, but the first worker will be ready for more work at time 101! On average, half our workers will be idle at any given time awaiting access to the index tuple. Note that, under the ideal circumstances assumed here, the performance of the code will improve in a well-behaved way up through 100 workers, then abruptly go flat[3]. If the user's understanding was based on an

---

[3]In the less-than-perfect real world, performance may degrade instead of flattening out—heavy contention for the index tuple may result in increased access time, making things even worse. The effect will likely kick in sooner than the ratio of average comparison time to access time would predict.

purely empirical study of the program's performance, there would be no warning that a performance collapse was imminent.

This problem needs to be dealt with pragmatically. Actual problems must be solved; problems that are merely "potential" need not be (and *should* not be, to the extent that a solution complicates the code or increases overhead at runtime). As we discuss in the performance section, for typical genetics database searches using a modest number of workers (under 100), there is no index-tuple bottleneck. For other forms of this problem, in other machine environments, there might be. A solution is obvious: use many index tuples instead of one.

> *Pop Quiz:* Develop a multiple-index program. Workers might be assigned to a sequence stream at initialization time, or they might choose streams dynamically. All streams can be fed by the same master or input process.

We've arrived at a realistic, practical solution to our search problem. Realistic, because we've used a strategy that will enable this code to handle virtually any size database. Practical because our program is highly parallel, and we've taken pains to ensure a reasonably good load balance.

We can install one final refinement, however. The actual constraints on `update_result()` are less severe than we've planned for. We collapsed two distinct jobs, result collation and output, into this one function. In the actual case of interest, we don't need to generate output for every result—just for the best (or n best) results, where n is much smaller than the total number of sequences. Hence we don't need to serialize the invocations of `update_result()` (or at least, we don't need to serialize them completely). We can migrate the update functionality from `update_result()` to `compare()` by having the latter keep track of the best result (or best n results) its worker has seen so far. When a worker's last task is complete, it reports its best results to the master. The master collects these local results and reduces them to one global result. The goal, of course, is to reduce the volume of data exchanged between the workers and the master (and the attendant overhead), and to parallelize the best-result computation.

Figures 6.4 and 6.5 presents the final database code. Workers use the **index** tuple to manage the task stream. The **result** tuple has now become two tuples, labelled **task done** and **worker done**. The first signals task completion to the master, for watermarking purposes; the second holds each worker's local maximum.

6.8 Performance analysis

While developing this code, we've made some isolated observations about various aspects of its performance. If we are to be reasonably sure that the code is working as designed, and in order to have some confidence in projecting its performance to other machines, we need to develop a model of its performance. We will proceed informally here, but the reader can carry this out to a surprisingly exact level of detail[4].

The serial code has two major components, the I/O and the comparisons. The I/O cost is essentially a linear function of the length of the database (we can ignore the target sequence for all "real" problems). The comparison cost is linear in the product of the lengths of the target and the database.

We've made no attempt to parallelize the I/O *per se*; rather, all I/O is done by the master in parallel with the worker's attack on the comparison tasks. Thus the amount of time spent on I/O is essentially the same in the serial and the parallel programs[5], but it will overlap with the computations. Likewise, each comparison takes the same amount of time it used to take (in the sequential version), but many comparisons will proceed in parallel. The parallel version bears the added cost of the Linda operations. If D is the number of sequences in the database and there are K workers, we'll need to do D outs in series, $D + K$ **in/outs**

---

[4]While much is made of nondeterminacy effects in parallel codes, the sort of codes being developed here, the underlying Linda implementations, and the hardware architectures are usually capable of delivering repeatable performance (within a few %). This is more than sufficient to permit study in enough detail to diagnose problems in the program (and even the occasional hardware glitch—a dead node on a 20 node shared memory machine is not immediately obvious but does become evident in careful performance testing).

[5]Of course, it probably won't be *exactly* the same, since the I/O pattern has changed from an input/compute cycle to input/out cycle with flow control.

```
char  dbe[MAX + HEADER],  target[MAX];
char  *dbs  =  dbe+HEADER;

real_main(argc,  argv)
        char                 **argv;
{
    t_length  =  get_target(argv[1],  target);
    open_db(argv[2]);
    num_workers  =  atoi(argv[3]);
    lower_limit  =  atoi(argv[4]);
    upper_limit  =  atoi(argv[5]);

    /* Set up. */
    for (i = 0;  i < num_workers;  ++i) eval("worker",  compare());
    out("target",  target:t_length);
    out("index",  1);

    /* Loop putting sequences into tuples. */
    tasks  =  0;
    task_id  =  0;
    while(d_length = get_seq(dbe)) {
        out("task",  ++task_id,  get_db_id(dbe),  dbs:d_length);
        if (++tasks > upper_limit)  /* Too many tasks, get some results. */
            do in("task done");  while (--tasks > lower_limit);
    }
    /* Poison tasks. */
    for (i = 0;  i < num_workers;  ++i) out("task",  ++task_id,  0,  "":0);
    close_db();

    while (tasks--) in("task done");    /* Clean up. */

    real_max  =  0;
    for (i = 0;  i < num_workers;  ++i) {    /* Get results. */
        in("worker done",  ? db_id,  ? max);
        if (real_max < max) {
            real_max  =  max;
            real_max_id  =  db_id;
        }
    }
    print_max(db_id,  real_max);
}
```

Figure 6.4
Database search: Final version, using streams (master).

```
char dbe[MAX + HEADER], target[MAX];
char *dbs = dbe+HEADER;

/* Work space for a vertical slice of the similarity matrix. * /
ENTRY_TYPE col_0[MAX+2], col_1[MAX+2], *cols[2]={col_0,col_1};

compare()
{
    SIDE_TYPE            left_side, top_side;

    rd("target", ? target:t_length);
    left_side.seg_start = target;
    left_side.seg_end = target + t_length;

    top_side.seg_start = dbs;

    local_max = 0;
    while (1) {
        in("index", ? task_id);
        out("index", task_id+1);
        in("task", task_id, ? db_id, ? dbs:d_length);

        /* If poison task, dump local max and exit. * /
        if (!d_length) break;

        /* Zero out column buffers. * /
        for (i=0; i <= t_length+1; ++i) cols[0][i]=cols[1][i]=ZERO_ENTRY;

        top_side.seg_end = dbs + d_length;
        max = 0;
        similarity(&top_side, &left_side, cols, 0, &max);
        out("task done");
        if (max > local_max) {
            local_max = max;
            local_max_id = db_id;
        }
    }
    out("worker done", local_max_id, local_max);
}
```

Figure 6.5
Database search: Final version (worker).

of the index tuple in series (although some of the in costs can be over-lapped with other ins and with one out), D ins of database sequences (in parallel), and K out/ins of result summaries (again overlapped to some extent). Assuming that D dominates K, we can lump all of these synchronization costs together into a single term, T_{Synch}, which will grow with D.

We assume that each worker ends up processing about the same total *length* of database sequences. (This assumption should be checked by collecting this datum for each worker and reporting it at the end of the computation.) Thus the runtime for the parallel version will be the maximum of three terms:

> *i)* t_{IO}, time needed to do the I/O (including outing the sequences and ining the results).

> *ii)* $t_{Seq}/K + t_{TO}(D/K)$, the parallelized execution time. t_{Seq} is the the sequential runtime. t_{TO} is the *parallelizable* part of the overhead associated with each task assignment. D is the number of tasks (that is, the number of sequences), and K is the number of workers (which must be $\leq D$).

> *iii)* $t_{Synch}D$, the non-parallelizable synchronization costs, where t_{Synch} is the per task *non-parallelizable* overhead.

Empirically, *ii* dominates the first and third expressions for "moderate" numbers of workers. We've discussed the program modifications (mul-tiple index-tuples and, possibly, parallel I/O) that are called for when large numbers of workers are deployed.

Figure 6.6 shows the speedup achieved by the program in figures 6.4 and 6.5. The graph shows speedup achieved by a given number of *workers* (not processes: the master is excluded) relative to a comparable se-quential program (*i.e.* a C, not a C-Linda program) running on a single processor of the machine at issue. The graph shows data obtained on an 18-processor Encore Multimax and a 64-processor Intel iPSC/2. (Recall that the Encore is a shared-memory and the Intel a distributed memory, hypercube-shaped parallel computer.) The test database contained 731 sequences totaling roughly 170,000 bases. The longest sequence was 468 bases; hence no single sequence dominates the computation on machines

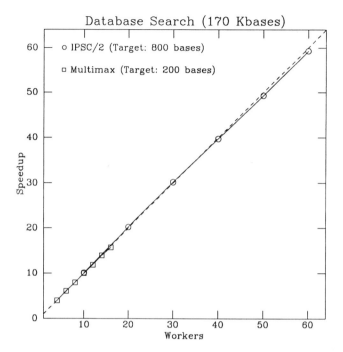

Figure 6.6
Speedup for the database search program.

with fewer than 360 processors. On the Multimax, we used a target sequence of length 200 bases. The sequential time was 661 seconds; our
C-Linda program ran in 42 seconds using 16 workers. The iPSC/2 runs
used a target of 800 bases: since this machine is about 4 times larger
than the Multimax, we increased the computation size by a factor of 4
to establish a comparable timing base when running with a full machine.
The sequential time was 2023 seconds; the C-Linda program using 60
workers ran in 34 seconds.

One final significant performance issue must be raised here, but can only
be resolved in the next chapter. We've discussed the ordering of tasks
by length-of-sequence in the interests of a good load balance. It's possible, though, that we might search a partition of the database whose
character is so pathological that a good load balance is *impossible* using the methods discussed in this chapter. It may be that the cost of

comparing a single very long sequence to the target dominates the cost of the entire remainder of the search. That is, if the first worker starts on this first comparison, and the rest set out through the remainder of the database, the first worker is still at it when the rest are finished. This situation is atypical for our database (as for most others), but under unlucky conditions it *can* occur. We discuss it further in the next chapter.

6.9   Conclusions

Problems with large quantities of obvious parallelism are often conveniently treated using the agenda paradigm. Such problems may be "embarrassingly parallel" (naturally endowed with very generous quantities of easily-recognized parallelism), but they may also be vitally important to significant computational efforts. For example, **Ray tracing.** This is an important technique for producing images in computer graphics. The general idea is to trace the path of a representative collection of light rays from the viewer's eyes backwards to the objects viewed and back again to the light source. Ray tracing can be parallelized in several ways—for example, by building separate pieces of the image (separate scan lines for a raster-display, for example) independently and simultaneously. Many other graphics and imaging techniques can also be parallelized. **Monte Carlo simulations** allow you to study the performance of a system (say a microchip exposed to potentially damaging radiation) by summing the effects of a large number of statistically-representative trials rather than by solving an equation that characterizes the system as a whole. Separate trials can often be computed simultaneously and independently. **Parameter sensitivity analyses** test a model's sensitivity to fluctuations in each of its input parameters; many trial runs using different parameter sets can often be computed simultaneously. The "model" might predict anything from the shape of a rocket plume to the behavior of the bond market. **Linkage analysis** is used to determine the most likely site on a chromosome for the genetic determinant of some trait, given information about how the trait is inherited relative to the inheritance of known genetic markers, and the layout of the chromosome. Many candidate sites can be investigated simultaneously.

This list could be extended nearly *ad infinitum*. The only thing these particular examples have in common is the fact that Linda has been used effectively to attack each of them.

Numerical computations that require repeated updates to a matrix are another set of good candidates for agenda parallelism. **LU decomposition**, for example, is a major step in the standard approach to solving sets of linear equations. It requires that a collection of matrix rows or columns be recomputed repeatedly; at each step in the iteration, all of these column-update computations can proceed simultaneously. The parallelization of direct methods for solving sparse systems of equations is a far more complicated problem, but it too can be approached using agenda parallelism [ACG89]. **Linear programming** using the simplex algorithm resembles LU decomposition in requiring a series of matrix updates which can be computed in parallel at each iteration. This is a small sample based (once again) on problems that have been solved using Linda; there are many other examples.

6.10 Exercises

The first four exercises involve a database search of the sort we've been discussing. To do them, you need a database and a search criterion. One interesting and easily-obtainable kind of database is a collection of text records. You can use files of email, for example, or of network news stories; or you can define a record as a single paragraph, and simply concatenate an arbitrary bunch of text files. Use any strategy you want, but build yourself a text database somehow or other. Next, you need a search criterion. One standard possibility is a scan for keywords or key phrases. Your search function accepts a predicate over words or phrases: for example, "find all records that include the phrases *gross national product, trade deficit, big seven, Japanese prime minister* or *speaking of capybaras...*" Keyword searches are usually implemented in terms of an elaborate index structure (which allows you to focus your attention on likely records only, avoiding an exhaustive scan); but they can be (and sometimes are) implemented in terms of an exhaustive search as well. Our assumption here is, of course, that you will perform an exhaustive search of the database; in this case, you'd return 1 when the predicate is satisfied and 0 otherwise. A better possibility is a search against an "interesting phrases (or words)" list. This might be an extensive list, kept in a file. Your search criterion returns a score: a higher score means a greater number of phrase matches.

1. Implement a search program against a text database. The user supplies a value that determines how many matches will be returned. If your criterion returns a score (not merely 1 or 0), records with the n best values are identified; otherwise *any* n records that match the predicate are identified. If the user supplies some distinguished value (say -1), *all* matches are returned. (If your criterion returns a score, they should be returned in sorted order.) Use a watermark scheme, but order the database by length only if performance requires.

If your records are short and your search criterion very simple, performance will be bad. (Why?) Try to build a better-performing version by using *clumping*: each task consists of searching a bunch of records instead of a single one.

2. Change your program so that it performs a cut-off search. There are two variants. If your criterion returns only 1 or 0, stop the program as soon as you've found n matches. (Execution should be shut down as expeditiously as possible. Note that it's not enough to out a poison pill that workers may just *happen* to ingest. They should swallow it at the earliest reasonable moment.) If your criterion returns a score, you'll have to examine every record in the database; but you should abort any search that is guaranteed to produce a worse value than the n best known so far ("so far" meaning "at the start of this comparison," not "right now").

3. Some vendors are now producing parallel machines with parallel I/O capabilities. Many more such machines will be available in future. Parallel I/O capabilities entail spreading a database over many disks, each attached to a different processor; hence we can perform many operations on the database simultaneously. Such capabilities are an obvious match to exactly the kind of parallel database search we've discussed in this chapter[6].

One way to adapt to the possibilities of parallel I/O is to build a database

---

[6]In fact, when Intel Scientific introduced its parallel I/O system in early 1989, they used a version of the Linda program described in this chapter to demo it.

searcher with multiple masters (or input processes). Each master runs on a processor with direct access to the database; all masters can read the database in parallel; they all feed the common bag or stream of tasks. Implement this version of your search program. (You won't necessarily have a parallel I/O system in fact, but you can experiment with this kind of logical structure regardless.)

Massive parallelism: 4. In the foreseeable future, asynchronous parallel machines encompassing tens of thousands of powerful processors (and more) will become available. Clearly, we can't feed thousands of workers from a single task *stream*; we've discussed multiple-stream search programs. It won't be practical to feed thousands of workers from the same task *bag* either. Although a bag requires no synchronization on access, current implementation techniques will break down in the face of tens of thousands of concurrent accesses to the same distributed data structure.

One interesting approach to the problem of massively parallel search involves a *hierarchy* of task bags or pools, with higher-level pools cascading into lower-level ones. The pools at the top of the hierarchy are fed by the master (or more likely by a collection of input processes, as discussed above). A cluster of sub-masters hovers beneath the top pool; each one is charged with replenishing its own second-level pool from the top pool as needed. Each second-level pool has a cluster of sub-sub-masters (brown belts?) clustered below *it*, and so on. The workers are located at the bottom of the hierarchy; each worker is assigned to some task pool. There are, of course, many such pools, each fed by its own local "master." Such a program structure lends itself to *multiple tuple space* versions of Linda, in which each pool can exist within a separate tuple space. But it's easily implemented in "standard" Linda as well. Implement it. For concreteness, assume that there is a single input process (a single top-level master, in other words, performing all file I/O), and at least two levels of sub-pools beneath the top pool.

This hierarchical approach can be applied to stream-based task management as well. A top-level ordered stream can feed second-level ordered streams, and so on. Implement this version as well.

□ 5. The oldest (probably) and best-established (certainly) notation for concurrency is the musical staff. The staff might be taken as a way of specifying *synchronous* parallelism only, but that's not quite so. True, tempo and (ordinarily) meter are the same for every line in the ensemble, and in a sense all threads are driven by a single clock. But of course, the separate musical lines in an ensemble do *not* proceed in lock-step. (*a*) Describe a notation for parallel programs that is based on musical notation. (Clearly you need to abstract some basic principles, not do a literal adaptation.) (*b*) Your notation provides a graceful way to express both specialist and agenda parallelism. Explain. (*c*) Use your notation to describe the relationship of the master to the workers in the database search program (with watermarking) described in this chapter.

7 Matrices: Starting with Result

In the previous chapter, we referred to a string-comparison algorithm for DNA sequences. The details of the algorithm weren't important, but we need to consider them now. The algorithm happens to be fairly typical of a broad class of important numerical problems: it requires the computation of a matrix in such a way that each matrix element depends either on the input data or on other, already-computed elements of the matrix[1]. We'll use this algorithm as the basis for our discussion of problems with natural result-parallel solutions.

In practical terms, we noted that the DNA database problem had two different kinds of solution: we could perform many sequential comparisons simultaneously, or we could parallelize each individual comparison. In this chapter we investigate the second approach. We then discuss, briefly, a third approach that incorporates elements from both the others. As in the previous chapter, the real topic (of course) isn't DNA sequence comparison; it's one significant type of parallel programming problem, its immediate *natural* solution, and the orderly transition from the *natural* solution to an *efficient* one—in other words, from the right starting place to a good stopping point.

7.1 Big issues

Main themes:

> *Load balance* is, again, crucial to good performance. The need for good load balance motivates our transformation from a result- to an agenda-parallel strategy.
>
> *Granularity control* is the other crucial issue. Here, we use the size of a matrix sub-block (see below) as a granularity knob.

---

[1] Not all DNA comparison algorithms work this way; but many algorithms in many domains do.

Special considerations:

Matrix sub-blocking is a powerful technique for building efficient matrix computations.

Logical inter-dependencies among sub-computations need to be understood and taken into account in building efficient programs. Here, we focus on an application with "wavefront" type dependencies.

7.2   Problem: the wavefront computation of a matrix

Given a function $h(x, y)$, we need to compute a matrix H such that the value in the *ith* row, *jth* column of H—that is, the value of $H[i, j]$ (in standard programming language notation) or $H_{i,j}$ (in mathematical notation)—is the function h applied to i and j, in other words $h(i, j)$.

The value of $h(i, j)$ depends on three other values: the values of $h(i - 1, j)$, of $h(i, j - 1)$ and of $h(i - 1, j - 1)$. To start off with, we're given the value of $h(0, j)$ for all values of j, and of $h(i, 0)$ for all values of i. These two sets of values are simply the *two strings that we want to compare*. In other words, we can understand the computation as follows: draw a two-dimensional matrix. Write one of the two comparands across the top and write the other down the left side. Now fill in the matrix; to fill in each element, you need to check the element on top, the element to the left, and the element on top and to the left.

7.3   The result-parallel approach

We noted in chapter two that *result parallelism is a good starting point for any problem whose goal is to produce a series of values with predictable organization and inter-dependencies.* What we've described is exactly such a problem.

Our computation fills in the entries of an $m \times n$ matrix (where m is, arbitrarily, the length of the shorter sequence and n is the length of the longer). Using result parallelism, we create a live data structure containing $m \times n$ processes, one for each element of the matrix. To do so we will execute a series of **eval** statements; to create the i, jth element of the live data structure, we execute a statement like

```
eval("H", i, j, h(i,j));
```

Here, h() is the function referred to above, charged with computing the i, jth entry on the basis of entries in the previous counter-diagonal of the matrix. Each process waits for its input values by blocking on **rd** statements. In general, the process that's computing entry (i, j) of the matrix will start out by executing

```
rd("H", i-1, j, ?val1);
rd("H", i, j-1, ?val2);
rd("H", i-1, j-1, ?val3);
```

It now performs an appropriate computation using values **val1**, **val2** and **val3** and completes, turning into the data tuple

```
("H", i, j,  the i,jth value of the matrix).
```

It's typical of the result paradigm that a simple outline like this is very close to the actual code. We need only add one detail. The matrix described above is the core of the computation, but for this problem the answer really isn't the matrix—it's the maximum value in the matrix. So we need to adjust slightly the concept of a matrix element and how to compute one. An element will now have a **value** field and a **max** field. After we have computed an element's **value**, we compute its **max** field. To do so, we simply take the maximum of (1) the **max** fields of each input element and (2) the newly-computed **value** of *this* element. It should be clear that the **max** field of the lower-right entry of the matrix will hold the maximum of *all* **values** in the matrix.

The result parallel code appears in figure 7.1 and 7.2. An entry's **value** actually consists of a triple (d, p, q), with d measuring similarity proper; these plus a **max** slot constitute the fields of each matrix entry. As discussed above, the answer (*i.e.* the maximum d value in the matrix) will be propagated to the **max** field of the lower-right entry. It is this entry that is ined at the end of **real_main**.

```
/* Adopted from O. Gotoh "An Improved Algorithm for Matching
   Biological Sequences", J. Mol. Biol. (162:pp705-708).
   This code is complete except for the constant MAX and the
   match_weight table. * /

typedef struct entry {
    int        d, max, p, q;
} ENTRY_TYPE;

ENTRY_TYPE zero_entry = { 0, 0, 0, 0};
#define ALPHA      4              /* indel penalty. * /
#define BETA       1              /* extension penalty. * /

char       side_seq[MAX], top_seq[MAX];

real_main(argc, argv)
        int             argc;
        char            **argv;
{
    ENTRY_TYPE          compare(), max_entry;
    int                 i, j;
    int                 side_len, top_len;

    side_len = get_target(argv[1], side_seq);
    top_len = get_target(argv[2], top_seq);

    for (i = 0; i < side_len; ++i)
       for (j = 0; j < top_len; ++j)
          eval("H", i, j, compare(i,j,side_seq[i],top_seq[j]));

    in("H", side_len-1, top_len-1, ? max_entry);

    printf("max: %d", max_entry.max);
}
```

Figure 7.1
A result-parallel wavefront matrix computation: main routine.

```
ENTRY_TYPE compare(i, j, b_i, b_j)
{
    ENTRY_TYPE       d, p, q;
    ENTRY_TYPE       me;
    int              t;

    d = p = q = zero_entry;
    if (i) rd("H", i-1, j, ? q);
    if (j) rd("H", i, j-1, ? p);
    if (i && j) rd("H", i-1, j-1, ? d);

    me.d = d.d + match_weights[b_i&0xF][b_j&0xF];
    if (me.d < 0) me.d = 0;

    me.p = p.d - ALPHA;
    t = p.p - BETA;
    if (me.p < t) me.p = t;

    me.q = q.d - ALPHA;
    t = q.q - BETA;
    if (me.q < t) me.q = t;

    if (me.p > me.d) me.d = me.p;
    if (me.q > me.d) me.d = me.q;

    /* Remember overall max. */
    me.max = me.d;
    if (d.max > me.max) me.max = d.max;
    if (p.max > me.max) me.max = p.max;
    if (q.max > me.max) me.max = q.max;

    return me;
}
```

Figure 7.2
The compare routine.

7.4   A result ⇒ agenda transformation

Our result parallel solution is simple and elegant, but its granularity
is too fine to allow efficient execution on most current-generation asynchronous multiprocessors. For starters, we are using three input values
to feed one very small computation. There is another cause of inefficiency as well, stemming from the data dependencies.

Consider the comparison of two 4-base sequences—the computation of a
4×4 matrix. At the starting point, only the upper-left matrix element
can be computed. Once this is done, the elements to its right and
beneath it (that is, the elements along the next counter-diagonal) can
be computed. In general, the enabled computations sweep down in a
wavefront from the upper-left element to the lower-right.

Suppose we look at the computation in terms of a series of discrete time
steps. During every step, everything that can be computed *is* computed.
We see that one element can be computed during the first time step,
two during the second, three during the third, and so on up through the
length of the longest diagonal. Thus, it's not until time step K that we
will have enough enabled tasks to keep K processors busy. The same
phenomenon occurs as the computation winds down. Opportunities for
parallel execution diminish until, at the last time step, only one element
remains to be computed. These start-up and shut-down phases limit
the amount of speedup we can achieve, and the efficiency with which
we can use our processors. For example, if we were to compare two
length-n sequences using n processors, the best speedup we could manage would be approximately $n/2$ (we are thus in effect throwing away
half our processors) – and this *ignores any other source of overhead*. In
practice, additional overhead is likely to reduce our achieved efficiency
to considerably less than 50%.

We'll have to address both the communication-to-computation ratio,
and the start-up and shut-down costs. A good way to address both will
be in terms of a transformation to an agenda-parallel approach. We can
transform the result parallel solution into an agenda-parallel approach
using essentially the same strategy we used in the primes-finder example.
We group the elements to be computed into bunches, and we create a
collection of worker processes. A single task is to compute all elements

in a bunch. A bunch of elements will be a sub-block of the matrix, as we'll describe below. This is the basic strategy, and it's fairly simple; but we need to deal with a number of details before we can make the strategy work effectively.

7.4.1 Granularity

We'll start with the issue of communication. In general, we want to do as much work as possible per communication event. Our strategy will be to enlarge each separate computation—to let the computation of many matrix elements, not just one, be the basic step. We can borrow a well-known technique of computational linear algebra in order to accomplish this. Many computations on matrices have the useful property that the computation can be easily rewritten to replace matrix elements with matrix sub-blocks, where a sub-block is merely a sub-matrix of elements contained within the original matrix. The wavefront computation we described above can easily be rephrased in terms of sub-blocks. We need to know how to handle each sub-block individually, and then how to handle *all* sub-blocks in the aggregate. Individually, each sub-block is treated in exactly the same way as the original matrix as a whole. In the aggregate, we can compute sub-blocks wavefront-by-wavefront, in exactly the same way we compute individual elements. A given sub-block is computed on the basis of known values for the three sub-blocks immediately above, to the left, and above and to the left. When we say "known values," though, we don't need to know these *entire* sub-blocks, merely the upper block's lower edge, the leftward block's right edge, and the bottom-right corner of the upper-left block. To eliminate the need for this one datum from the upper-left block, we can define blocks in such a way that that they overlap their neighbors by one row or column. Hence we can compute a new sub-block on the basis of one row (from above) and one column (from the left).

Assuming for the moment that we have square $n \times n$ sub-blocks, we have two communication events each involving $n + 1$ pieces of data supporting the n^2 computations that are required to fill-in a sub-block. We can control granularity by controlling the size of n. The ratio of communication to computation falls as we increase the size of the sub-blocks.

Of course, increasing sub-block size has an obvious disadvantage as well. Consider the extreme case. If the sub-block is the entire matrix, we succeed in eliminating communication costs altogether—and with them, all available parallelism! As we increase the block size, we improve prospects for "local" efficiency (each task has less relative overhead) but we may reduce "global" efficiency by producing too few tasks to keep all processors busy. Nonetheless, we now have a granularity knob that we can adjust to give a reasonable tradeoff between the two extremes of many small tasks with relatively large communication overheads and one large task with no communication overhead.

7.4.2   An agenda-style solution

We *could* build a result-parallel program based on sub-block rather than single-element computations (see the exercises). But there's an efficiency problem in our computation that is conveniently handled by switching to a master-worker model.

Our computation has start-up and shut-down phases. Having divided our matrix into sub-blocks, we could create one process for each sub-block (that is, we could build a live data structure). But many of these processes would be inactive for much of the time. In general, the parallelism we can achieve is limited by the length of the longest diagonal (*i.e.* the length of the shorter of the two sequences being compared): at no time can there be more enabled computations than elements in the longest diagonal. But if this length is k, and we have k processors, all k processors will be active only during the middle of the computation. We can get better efficiencies (at the cost of some degree of *absolute* speedup, of course) by executing with fewer than k processors.

If efficiency is important, then, we will run with far fewer processors than there are sub-blocks in the matrix. We face, once again, a load-balancing problem. We could write a result-parallel program under the assumption that the underlying system will balance enabled processes correctly among available processors. We might begin with a random assignment of processes to processors, and simply move processes around at runtime from heavily- to lightly-burdened processors. But this is difficult to accomplish on parallel processors that lack shared memory— for example on hypercubes, Transputer arrays or local area networks.

In such distributed-memory environments, moving a process requires copying the entire process image from one address space to another. This *can* be done—but at the expense of some complex operating system support, and the obvious runtime costs of moving process images around.

A more conservative approach is to *abstract,* and thereby make the switch to an agenda-parallel, master-worker scheme. A task will be the computation of a single sub-block (with a qualification to be discussed below). The naturally load-balancing properties of this software structure work in favor of an efficient implementation.

> *Massive parallelism:* Some of the assumptions behind these arguments will almost certainly be falsified on future massively parallel asynchronous machines. These machines should provide communication support that's fast enough to relieve us from many of our current concerns about fine-grained programs. In such a setting, program development could have stopped several paragraphs ago, with the pure result solution. Result parallelism seems like an excellent way to express matrix computations for massively parallel computers.
>
> Given a sufficiently large parallel machine, throwing away processors in the interests of strong absolute performance might be an excellent strategy. If D (the length of the longest diagonal) represents the maximum achievable degree of parallelism, you may insist on getting D-way parallelism whatever efficiencies you achieve—despite the fact (in other words) that many processors are idle during start-up and shut-down. Even if you have processors to burn, though, you won't necessarily want to waste them needlessly. You may unwilling to use *more* than D processors.
>
> To program such a machine, you might build a length-D vector of processes. Each process in the vector computes every element in its row. It leaves a stream of tuples behind, representing the first element in its row, the second element and so on. The second process in the vector can begin as soon as the first process's stream is one element long, and so on. The resulting program is more complex than the result-parallel

version given above, but it's simple and elegant nonetheless. (See the exercises.)

Another possible approach is to apply existing automatic transformation techniques to our pure result program, producing in effect the same sort of D-process program we've just discussed. The transformation techniques developed by Chen in the context of her Crystal compiler [Che86] might be applicable here[2].

7.4.3   What should the sub-blocks look like?

So, we've designed a master-worker program where a task is the computation of a single matrix sub-block. We must now consider what a sub-block should look like.

Notice that, if we are comparing two sequences of *different* lengths, potential efficiency improves. The shorter-sized sequence determines the maximum degree of parallelism. But whereas, for a square result matrix, full parallelism is achieved during a single time step only (namely the time-step during which we compute the elements along the longest counter-diagonal), a rectangular matrix sustains full parallelism over many time steps. The difference between the lengths of the longer and the shorter sequence is the number of additional time steps during which maximum parallelism is sustained.

Suppose our two sequences are length m (the shorter one) and n, and suppose we are executing the program with m workers. The number of time steps for parallel execution, t_{par}, is given by

$$2m + (n - (m - 1)),$$

so for $m, n \gg 1$

$$t_{par} \approx m + n.$$

---

[2]These techniques are currently targeted at functional-language programs, and functional languages are unacceptable for our purposes; they may support a neat solution to the problem discussed here, but outside the bounds of this chapter they fall flat. Like parallel do-loop languages, they are too inflexible to be attractive tools; we want to solve many sorts of problems, not just one. *But*—Chen's techniques may well be applicable outside of the constricting functional language framework.

The sequential time, t_{seq}, is given by $m * n$, and thus speedup, S, is

$$\frac{t_{seq}}{t_{par}} = \frac{mn}{m+n}.$$

Note that if $n \gg m$,

$$S \approx m.$$

In other words, if $n \gg m$, we get essentially perfect speedup (m workers yielding a speedup of m), and perfect efficiency. This result is intuitively simple and reasonable. Picture a short (in height), wide (in width) matrix—a matrix for which $n \gg m$. It has *many* longest counter-diagonals (where a square matrix has only one). Each counter-diagonal is m long; whenever we are computing a counter-diagonal, we can use all m workers at once, and thus get m-fold speedup. If we define the *aspect ratio*, α, of a matrix to be the ratio of its width to its height, then

$$\alpha = \frac{n}{m}$$

and

$$S = \left(\frac{\alpha}{\alpha + 1} \right) m.$$

So, if α happens to be 10 (one sequence is ten times longer than the other), efficiency can be as high as 90%.

Combining this observation with the concept of blocking yields a mechanism for controlling start-up and shut-down costs. We've been assuming that sub-blocks are square (although we do have to allow for odd shaped blocks along the right edge and the bottom). But they don't have to be. We have an additional, important degree of freedom in designing this program: the aspect ratio of a sub-block (as opposed to that of the whole matrix). We can use non-square sub-blocks to produce a blocked matrix just high enough to make use of all available workers, but long enough to reduce start-up and shut-down inefficiencies to an acceptable level. In other words, we can set the aspect ratio of a matrix (in its blocked form) by adjusting the aspect ratio of its sub-blocks.

First, we choose an ideal height for our sub-blocks. If our blocked matrix is exactly W high (where W is the number of worker processes), then each worker can compute a single row of the blocked matrix. To achieve a W-high blocked matrix, we set the height of each sub-block to m (the length of the shorter sequence, hence the height of the original matrix) divided by W. We now need to determine a good width for each sub-block. Let's say that we aim for an efficiency of 90%. For a maximum-achievable efficiency of 90%, α (as we saw above) should be ≈ 10. It follows that each row of the blocked matrix should have $10W$ elements. Hence, the width of of a sub-block should be the length of the longer sequence divided by $10W$.

Why not shoot for 95% efficiency?

> *Pop quiz:* What α corresponds to 95% efficiency? 99% efficiency?

Keep in mind that the number of communication events (transfers of a sub-block's bottom edge from one worker to the worker directly below) grows linearly with α. Too much communication means bad performance.

7.4.4   Task scheduling

A task—the computation of a sub-block—is enabled once the sub-blocks to its left and above it have been computed. (Sub-blocks along the top and the leftmost rim depend on one neighbor only, of course; the upper-left sub-block depends on no others.) Clearly, we can't merely dump task-descriptors for every sub-block into a bag at the start of the computation, and turn the workers loose. We must ensure that workers grab a task-descriptor only when the corresponding task is enabled.

We *could* begin with a single enabled task (the computation of the upper-left block), and arrange for workers to generate other tasks dynamically as they become enabled. (See the exercises.) Another solution is (in some ways) simpler. After a worker computes a sub-block, it proceeds to compute the next sub-block to the right. Thus, the first worker starts cruising across the top band of the matrix, computing sub-blocks. As soon as the upper-left sub-block is complete, the second worker can start cruising across the second band. When this second worker is done with its own left-most sub-block, the third worker starts cruising across the third band, and so on.

This scheme has several advantages. We've simplified scheduling, and reduced task-assignment overhead: once a worker has been given an initial task assignment, the assignment holds good for an entire row's worth of blocks. We have also reduced inter-process communication overhead. When a block is complete, its right and bottom edges will, in general, be required by other computations. Under our band-cruising scheme, though, there's no need to drop a newly-computed right-edge into tuple space. No other worker will ever need to pick it up; the worker that generated it will use it.

We present the code for this version in figures 7.3 and 7.4. The partitioning of the matrix into sub-blocks of nearly equal height is a bit obscure. Since the number of workers may not evenly divide the lengths of the sequences, we must provide for slightly non-uniform blocks. We could treat the left-over as a lump forming one final row and column of blocks smaller than the rest. But this would leave the worker assigned to the last row with less work than all the rest, leading to an unnecessary efficiency loss. Instead, we increment the height (or width—see the worker's code) by 1, and use this larger value until all the excess has been accounted for, at which point we decrement the height to its "correct" value.

The worker code uses the `similarity()` routine from the previous chapter. We can now account for its extra arguments. It's designed to accept a pointer to a `max` value (for recording the maximum entry computed), working buffers (`cols`), a description of the sequence segments that label the left and top sides of a sub-block, and a vector of entries forming the top edge of the sub-block. During the computation, this vector is overwritten with a new set of values defining the *bottom* edge of the sub-block. The `cols` buffer are used in analogous fashion: initially `cols[0]` points to a buffer holding the left edge, finally it points to the buffer holding the right edge of the sub-block. Thus, when `similarity()` completes, we know the maximum similarity value within the sub-block, and the values that define the right and bottom edges.

The program's performance is summarized by the speedup graph in figure 7.5 (as usual, the abscissa reports the number of workers—the number of processes is one greater). We ran tests on the Encore Multimax and the Intel iPSC/2, again running a larger problem on the larger Intel machine. On both machines, α (the aspect ratios) was 10. Again,

```
char          side_seq[MAX],  top_seq[MAX];

real_main(argc,  argv)
        char            **argv;
{
   char                *sp;

   side_len  =  get_target(argv[1],  side_seq);
   top_len  =  get_target(argv[2],  top_seq);
   num_workers  =  atoi(argv[3]);
   aspect_ratio  =  atoi(argv[4]);

   /* Set up. * /
   for (i = 0;  i < num_workers;  ++i) eval("worker",  compare());
   out("top sequence",  top_seq:top_len);

   height  =  side_len  /  num_workers;
   left_over  =  side_len  −  (height*num_workers);

   ++height;
   for (i = 0,  sp = side_seq;  i < num_workers;  ++i, sp += height) {
      if (i == left_over)  −−height;
      out("task",  i,  num_workers,  aspect_ratio,  sp:height);
   }

   real_max  =  0;
   for (i = 0;  i < num_workers;  ++i) {
      in("result",  ? max);
      if (max > real_max)    real_max  =  max;
   }
   print_max(real_max);
}
```

Figure 7.3
Wavefront: The agenda-parallel version (master).

```
char side_seq[MAX], top_seq[MAX]; /*Note: MAX can differ from main.* /

/* Work space for a vertical slice of the similarity matrix. * /
ENTRY_TYPE col_0[MAX+2], col_1[MAX+2], *cols[2]={col_0,col_1};
ENTRY_TYPE top_edge[MAX];

compare()
{
    SIDE_TYPE          left_side, top_side;

    rd("top sequence", ? top_seq:top_len);
    top_side.seg_start = top_side.seq_start;

    in("task", ? id, ? num_workers, ? aspect_ratio, ? side_seq:height);
    left_side.seg_start = side_seq;
    left_side.seg_end = left_side.seg_start + height;

    /* Zero out column buffers. * /
    for (i = 0; i <= height+1; ++i) cols[0][i]=cols[1][i]=ZERO_ENTRY;

    max = 0;
    blocks = aspect_ratio*num_workers;
    width = top_len / blocks;
    left_over = top_len − (width*blocks);
    ++width;
    /* Loop across top sequence, stride is width of a sub−block. * /
    for (block_id = 0;
            block_id < blocks;
            ++block_id, top_side.seg_start += width) {
        if (block_id == left_over) −−width;
        top_side.seg_end = top_side.seg_start + width;

        if (id)             /* Get top edge from the worker "above". * /
            in("top edge", id, block_id, ? top_edge:);
        else                /* If nothing above, use zero. * /
            for (i = 0; i < width; ++i) top_edge[i] = ZERO_ENTRY;

        similarity(&top_side, &left_side, cols, top_edge, &max);

        /* Send "bottom" edge (in reality the overwritten top_edge). * /
        if ((id+1) < num_workers)
            out("top edge", id+1, block_id, top_edge:width);
    }
    out("result", max);
}
```

Figure 7.4
Wavefront: The agenda-parallel version (worker).

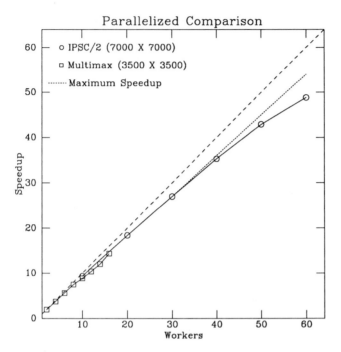

Figure 7.5
Speedup for the agenda-parallel version.

speedup is relative to a sequential C program running on one processor of the machine in question.

On the Multimax, our test problem compared a sequence of length 3500 against itself[3] The Multimax sequential time for this problem was 258 seconds... or 247 seconds. Here we have an example of the memory effects discussed in chapter 4. These large sequences are "cache busters" taken in their entirety, but will fit in cache when they're broken up into pieces. The higher sequential time (258 seconds) is the figure actually reported by the sequential code. The lower time is calculated by extrapolation from the sequential database-search times—recall that, for the problems discussed in the previous chapter, the sequences in the

---

[3]Big problems are what we want to parallelize; here, a big problem is a big sequence (not a big database). The largest sequence in just one subset of the standard compendium of genetic sequence data is, at present, over 70,000 bases long; there's nothing implausible about a length 3500 sequence.

database and the target sequences are all "small" compared with our current test case. Which time should we use in assessing performance? The former is of more interest to the program's user. But the latter corrects for memory effects, and thus makes it somewhat easier to assess our analysis and verify our understanding of this code's performance. Setting α to 10 should yield a maximum-achievable speedup that is 90% of ideal. And indeed, using the lower (memory-effect corrected) time, our measured efficiencies are within 5% of this model through 10 workers on the Multimax and 40 workers on the iPSC/2. (Using the larger time, efficiencies *exceed* the "maximum achievable" figure on both machines for small numbers of workers.)

The 16-worker time for the Multimax was 18 seconds. Using a 7000-base self-comparison problem, sequential times for the iPSC/2 were 776 and 758 seconds; 60 workers finished the computation in 16 seconds. On both machines, there is a tail-off in efficiency as the number of workers increases. We can account for this tail-off if we think about the size of each block as a function of the number of workers. The number of blocks is α times the square of the number of workers; thus, the size of each block, and accordingly the amount of work per communication event, *falls as the square of the number of workers.* It is the inexorable drag arising from this steadily-sinking task granularity that shows up in the observed performance degradation.

7.5   Back to the original database problem

We've developed a reasonable approach to parallel wavefront computations. Suppose, though, that we need to perform a *series* of wavefront computations—not merely a single one in isolation. Why should a series of computations be necessary? For one, consider our original DNA-database problem. Our goal was to compare a target to every sequence in the database, not merely to one other sequence.

One way to speedup a series of events is (of course) to speedup each event in the series. In this sense, parallelizing each individual comparison, using the techniques developed in this chapter, is one way to speedup the database search as a whole. But once we've decided to perform a whole series of comparisons, a further significant optimization to our wavefront technique suggests itself.

The idea is simply to overlap the shut-down phase for one comparison with the start-up phase for the next. Processors that would normally lie idle while the last few sub-blocks of one comparison were being computed can be set to work on the first few sub-blocks of the next comparison. As a result, we pay *once* for start-up and *once* for shut-down over the *entire* database search.

The conversion to overlapped execution is simple in principle, but we must take care to avoid several problems. First, there need only be two sequences (or actually, parts of two sequences) in tuple space at any point; again, we must assume that our database is too large to fit into core, and that we must play it out gradually. While some workers finish up one comparison, the rest soldier on to begin the next. Carrying out this clutter-control strategy requires some additional synchronization between the master and the workers. Our code uses an `index` tuple to assign each worker an identification tag for the duration of a particular sequence comparison. (The id is, in effect, the index of the row for which the worker will be responsible.) The worker who picks up the last id (`num_workers-1`) informs the master that all workers have signed on to the most recent comparison. Only then does the master set up the *next* comparison.

The second problem is a bit more subtle. If we are not careful to distinguish `top edge` tuples, the possibility exists that tuples from two different comparisons might be mixed up. A speedy first worker might romp through the first row of one comparison strewing `top edge` tuples for the second row in its wake, and then zip on to the first row of the next comparison. If the worker handling the second row of the first comparison is relatively slow, it may see a mixture of `top edge` tuples, some from the first comparison and some from the second. Thus, block coordinates alone are insufficient labels for `top edge` data; we need to include a `task_id` as well. This change is easily handled by adding a `task_id` field to the `top edge` tuple.

The code, reflecting these comments, is given in figures 7.6 and 7.7.

We noted in the previous section that our blocking approach has a drawback: task granularity falls as the square of the number of workers.

```
char        dbe[MAX + HEADER], dbs=dbe + HEADER, target[MAX];

real_main(argc, argv)
      char          **argv;
{
   char             *dbsp;

   t_length = get_target(argv[1], target);
   open_db(argv[2]);
   num_workers = atoi(argv[3]);

   /* Set up. */
   for (i = 0; i < num_workers; ++i) eval("worker", compare());
   out("top sequence", num_workers, target:t_length);

   while (d_length = get_seq(dbe)) {
      out("id", 0);

      height = d_length / num_workers;
      left_over = d_length - (height*num_workers);
      ++height;
      for (i = 0, dbsp = dbs; i < num_workers; ++i, dbsp += height) {
         if (i == left_over) --height;
         out("task", i, ++task_id, get_db_id(dbe), dbsp:height);
      }
      in("started");
   }
   for (i = 0; i < num_workers; ++i) out("id", -1);

   /* Gather maxes local to a given worker and compute global max. */
   real_max = 0;
   for (i = 0; i < num_workers; ++i) {
      in("result", ? db_id, ? max);
      (max > real_max) ? (real_max=max, real_max_id=db_id):0;
   }
   print_max(db_id, real_max);
}
```

Figure 7.6
Overlapped database search (master).

```
/* side_seq, top_seq, col_0, etc., are the same as in figure FOO. * /
compare()
{
    SIDE_TYPE          left_side, top_side;

    rd("top sequence", ? num_workers, ? top_seq:top_len);
    width = top_len /num_workers;
    left_over = top_len - (width*num_workers);

    local_max = 0;
    while (1) {
        in("id", ?id);
        if (id == -1) break;
        ((id+1) == num_workers) ? out("started") : out("id", id+1);

        in("task", id, ? task_id, ? db_id, ? side_seq:height);
        if (height == 0) break;

        top_side.seg_start = top_seq;
        left_side.seg_start = side_seq;
        left_side.seg_end = left_side.seg_start + height;
        for (i = 0; i <= height+1; ++i) cols[0][i]=cols[1][i]=ZERO_ENTRY;

        /* Loop across top sequence, stride is width of a sub-block. * /
        ++width;
        max = 0;
        for (block_id = 0; block_id < num_workers;
                ++block_id, top_side.seg_start += width) {
            if (block_id == left_over) --width;
            top_side.seg_end = top_side.seg_start + width;

            if (id)            /* Get top edge from the worker "above". * /
                in("top edge", task_id, id, block_id, ? top_edge:);
            else               /* If nothing above, use zero. * /
                for (i = 0; i < width; ++i) top_edge[i] = ZERO_ENTRY;

            similarity(&top_side, &left_side, cols, top_edge, &max);

            /* Send "bottom" edge (in reality the overwritten top_edge). * /
            if ((id+1) < num_workers)
                out("top edge", task_id, id+1, block_id, top_edge:width);
        }
        (max > local_max) ? (local_max=max, local_max_id=db_id):0;
    }
    out("result", local_max_id, local_max);
}
```

/* Exercise: why can't we make "started" == "id", num_workers ? * /

Figure 7.7
Overlapped database search (worker).

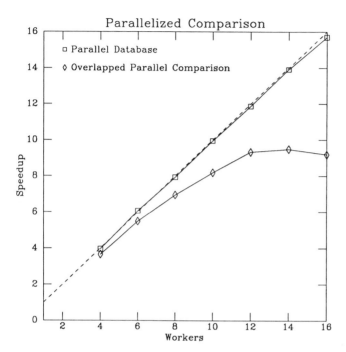

Figure 7.8
"Standard" database search *vs.* overlapped search.

This means the code is likely to be efficient only when dealing with relatively large sequences or running with relatively few workers. In our test database, short sequences predominate. Figure 7.8 compares the speedup using the overlapping code to speedup for the final version of the code in the previous chapter, using the test case described there for the Multimax. As the number of workers increases, speedup is acceptable at first, then levels off, and then actually begins (at 16 workers) to *decrease*. Nonetheless, for a modest number of workers, overlapping *does* work. α is 1 here, and yet we manage a speedup of over 9 with 12 workers, *versus* an expected speedup of 6 using the wavefront code "as is" to process a series of comparisons.

7.6   And the denouement: hybrid search

We've made a number of changes to the original code that have resulted in a much more efficient program. We can also see that this code doesn't suffer from many of the problems that the agenda version did. In particular because it parallelizes each comparison we needn't worry about the issues stemming from the multiple comparison approach of the agenda version: we only need one sequence (or a few sequences) from the database at any given time, we don't need to order the sequences to improve load balancing, and long comparisons will not lead to idle workers. So why bother with the other version? In a word, efficiency. Doing comparisons in chunks *must* involve more overhead than doing them "whole". Ideally we would like to pay that overhead only when necessary, and use the parallel comparisons of the previous chapter (as opposed to *parallelized* comparisons) by default. Fortunately, it's possible to write a code that combines the best parts of both.

Actually, we've already done it (almost). The hybrid approach follows from a simple observation: if we could fix the block size by making it relatively large, comparisons involving long sequences would still be blocked (and therefore be "internally" parallelized), while short sequences would fit into one block, with many such comparisons taking place in parallel. In other words, we would use the more efficient approach where it worked best: with moderate size comparisons. We would use the more expensive approach where it was needed: for very long sequences.

To do this we need to modify our previous code to manage tasks explicitly—we can no longer guarantee that all workers are meshing together in the same they did for the overlapped code, in which sub-blocking was adjusted to ensure every worker had a slice of every comparison. We can still exploit row affinity, so this boils down to handling the first sub-block of each row as task that when created is "incomplete" and that becomes enabled when the the the top-edge is computed.

We must now choose an appropriate block size. If sub-blocks are too large, the largest piece of work may still dominate the rest of the computation. If they are too small, we defeat our attempt to use more efficient whole-sequence (*non*-sub-blocked) comparisons whenever possible.

To simplify things, let's assume that the target sequence always defines the top row of the comparison matrix and that there is at least one really large sequence that needs blocking (a worst case assumption). The largest possible chunk of work, then, is the computation of a row of sub-blocks. The size of this chunk *in toto* is $T * B$, where T (the width) is the length of the target, and B (the height) is the height of one block. To this point, we've neglected start-up and shut-down costs; if we add these in, the *last* piece of work this size cannot be completed any earlier than the time needed to compute about $2TB$ entries, establishing a lower limit for the parallel runtime. If the total number of workers is W, we would like maximum speedup to be W, or in other words

$$S = W = \frac{DT}{2TB} = \frac{D}{2B},$$

where D is the size of the database. This in turn implies that

$$B = \frac{D}{2W}.$$

Note that this constraint is easily expressed algebraically and straightforward to compute. Thus it's no problem to design a code that dynamically adapts to information about the number of processors (which implies the desired speedup) and the size of the database. Once again, we have a knob that can be used to adjust the granularity of tasks to suit the resources at hand.

The code, assuming a constant block size, is presented in figures 7.9 and 7.10.

Once again, we present performance data for the Multimax and iPSC/2. First, to establish that this code is competitive with last chapter's simpler database code, figure 7.11 compares speedups for this program and the the chapter 6 program using the same test database as before. As expected, there's virtually no difference. To illustrate the problem we're addressing, figure 7.12 presents speedups for these same two programs on the iPSC/2 when our test database is augmented by a single 19,000-base sequence. The 19 Kbase whopper imposes a maximum speedup of about 9 on the database code; the speedup data clearly demonstrate this upper bound. The hybrid version, on the other hand, takes the big sequence in stride. It delivers close to the same speedup as it did in the previous case.

```
char dbe[MAX + HEADER], *dbs = dbe+HEADER, target[MAX];

real_main(argc, argv)
        char          **argv;
{
    char              *dbsp;

    t_length = get_target(argv[1], target);
    open_db(argv[2]);
    num_workers = atoi(argv[3]);
    lower_limit = atoi(argv[4]);
    upper_limit = atoi(argv[5]);

    /* Set up. */
    for (i = 0; i < num_workers; ++i) eval("worker", compare());
    out("top sequence", target:t_length);
    out("index", 1);

    while (d_length = get_seq(dbe)) {
        blocks = (d_length+BLOCK-1) /BLOCK;
        if (blocks > t_length) blocks = t_length;
        height = d_length / blocks;
        left_over = d_length - (height*blocks);
        ++height;
        for (i = 0, dbsp = dbs; i < blocks; ++i, dbsp += height) {
            if (i == left_over) --height;
            out("task", ++task_id, i, blocks, get_db_id(db_id), dbsp:height);
        }
        if (++tasks > upper_limit) /* Too many tasks, get some results. */
            do in("task done"); while (--tasks > lower_limit);
    }
    /* Poison tasks. */
    for (i = 0; i < num_workers; ++i) out("task", ++task_id, -1,0,0,"":0);
    close_db();

    while (tasks--) in("task done"); /* Clean up. */

    /* Gather maxes local to a given worker and compute global max. */
    real_max = 0;
    for (i = 0; i < num_workers; ++i) {
        in("result", ? db_id, ? max);
        (max > real_max) ? (real_max=max, real_max_id=db_id):0;
    }
    print_max(db_id, real_max);
}


/* Remark: BLOCK could be a function of |DB| and num_workers:
   block = |DB| /(2*nw) */
```

Figure 7.9
Hybrid database search (master).

```
/* side_seq, top_seq, col_0, etc., are the same as in figure FOO. */
compare()
{
    SIDE_TYPE            left_side, top_side;

    rd("top sequence", ? top_seq:top_len);

    local_max = 0;
    while (1) {
        in("index", ? task_id);
        out("index", task_id+1);
        in("task", task_id, ? id, ? blocks, ? db_id, ? side_seq:height);
        if (id == -1) break;

        top_side.seg_start = top_seq;
        left_side.seg_start = side_seq;
        left_side.seg_end = left_side.seg_start + height;
        for (i = 0; i <= height+1; ++i) cols[0][i]=cols[1][i]=ZERO_ENTRY;

        /* Loop across top sequence, stride is width of a sub-block. */
        width = top_len /blocks;
        left_over = top_len - (width*blocks);
        ++width;
        max = 0;
        for (block_id = 0; block_id < blocks;
                ++block_id, top_side.seg_start += width){
            if (block_id == left_over) —width;
            top_side.seg_end = top_side.seg_start + width;

            if (id)             /* Get top edge from the worker "above". */
                in("top edge", task_id, block_id, ? top_edge:);
            else                /* If nothing above, use zero. */
                for (i = 0; i < width; ++i) top_edge[i] = ZERO_ENTRY;

            similarity(&top_side, &left_side, cols, top_edge, &max);

            /* Send "bottom" edge (in reality the overwritten top_edge). */
            if ((id+1)<blocks) out("top edge",task_id+1,block_id,top_edge:width);
        }
        (max > local_max) ? (local_max=max, local_max_id=db_id):0;
        out("task done");
    }
    out("result", local_max_id, local_max);
}
```

Figure 7.10
Hybrid database search (worker).

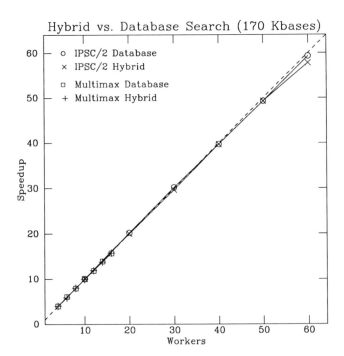

Figure 7.11
"Standard" database search *vs.* hybrid search.

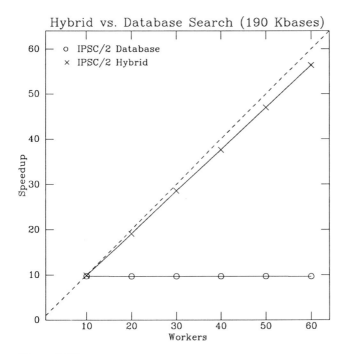

Figure 7.12
The same search, over a test database augmented with a 19 Kbase jumbo sequence.

7.7   Conclusions

Many other computations can be approached using the techniques described in the chapter. Any problem that can be described in terms of a recurrence relation belongs in this category. Matrix arithmetic falls into this category; we discuss **matrix multiplication** in the exercises.

The result itself needn't be a matrix; we might, for example, build a parallel program in the shape of a tree that develops dynamically as the program runs. Tree-based algorithms like **travelling salesman** and **alpha-beta search** are candidates for this kind of result parallelism; so are parsers of various kinds.

7.8   Exercises

1. **Matrix multiplication** is a problem that can be treated in roughly the same way as string comparison (although it's much simpler, with no inter-element dependencies). Multiplying a $p \times q$ matrix A by a $q \times r$ matrix B yields a $p \times r$ matrix C, where the value of $C[i, j]$ is the inner product of the *ith* row of A and the *jth* column of B. To get the inner product of two vectors, multiply them pairwise and add the products: that is, add the product of the two first elements plus the product of the two second elements and so on.

Write a result-parallel matrix multiplication routine (it assumes that the two matrices to be multiplied are stored one element per tuple). Clearly, all elements of the result can be computed simultaneously. In principle, the multiplications that are summed to yield each inner product could also be done simultaneously—but don't bother; they can be done sequentially. Now, transform your result-parallel code into an efficient master-worker program that uses sub-blocking. (The input matrices will now be assumed to be stored one block per tuple, and the result will be generated in this form as well.)

2. (a) Write the vector-based result parallel string-comparison program described in the "massive parallelism" discussion above. Each process can turn into a data tuple, before it does so creating a new process to compute the next element in its row; or, each row can be computed by

a single process that creates a stream of data tuples. (*b*) We've assumed that a "live vector" is created as a first step. The vector's first element starts computing immediately; the other elements are blocked, but unblock incrementally as the computation proceeds. Write a (slightly) different version in which you begin with a *single* process (which computes the first row of the result); the first process creates the second process as soon it's finished computing one element; the second process creates the third, and so on.

3. Write a result-parallel string comparison program with adjustable granularity. (Each process will compute an entire sub-block of the result.)

4. Write a different version of the agenda-parallel string comparison program. Workers don't cruise along rows, computing each sub-block; instead, they grab any enabled task from tuple space. An enabled task is a sub-block whose input elements (the values along its left and upper edge) have already been computed. Compare the code-complexity and (if possible) the performance of the two versions. How would this strategy affect the overlapped and hybrid searches?

8 Networks: Starting with Specialist

Consider the following problem: you need a data-stream analysis program—further on, we will discuss a variant in which the problem is a *realtime* data-analysis program. Incoming streams of data are to be converted into a high-level synopsis or overview of the situation being described by the data streams. For example: data streams generated by medical monitoring equipment in an intensive care unit describe the patient's blood pressure, heart rate, temperature and many other vital signs; what does it all mean? What is the patient's condition? Is he getting better or worse? Data streams generated by avionics equipment describe an airplane's current situation—is the current situation satisfactory, optimal? Are there problems that the pilot should be worrying about? Data streams describe the condition of a complex market (a stock exchange, for example)—where is the market going? And incidentally, is insider trading going on? Data streams describe current atmospheric conditions; what's the weather, and which way is it tending? There are many other examples. Software to solve this kind of data-analysis problem is likely to become extremely important in the near future.

8.1 Big issues

Main themes:

> *Load balance* again is a main issue, and motivates our transformation from a specialist- to an agenda-parallel strategy.

Special considerations:

> *Agenda-parallel programs may be simpler than specialist-parallel programs* even where network-structured programs are involved. Using abstraction to transform a process graph into a set of node-states that can be updated by workers in

parallel may allow us to localize all interconnections to a single process, instead of distributing them throughout the program.

A *realtime constraint*—the necessity of assuring that a computation can be completed within some fixed period—imposes special scheduling requirements. We may be forced to seek a static task schedule, instead of relying on dynamic tasking.

8.2   The data-stream analysis problem

Our main focus in this chapter is a particular *software architecture* designed with the data-analysis problem in mind. A software architecture is a structural framework for software—a plan that shows the basic module structure of a program, and the strategy for connecting the modules together. The software architecture we'll use to solve the data-analysis problem is the *process trellis*.

The trellis architecture is based on a hierarchical graph of decision processes. Each process concentrates on one part of the problem. We can break most data-analysis problems into pieces in such a way that some pieces are "low-level", others "high-level" and others in between. Low-level pieces generally focus on a particular data stream; high-level pieces attempt to answer a general question about the situation. If we are monitoring patients in an intensive care unit, for example, a low-level process might concentrate on figuring out whether heart rate is stable or is trending higher or lower; a high-level process might concentrate on a question like "is the patient suffering from septic shock (or some other disease)—or moving closer to this condition?" Medium-level processes concentrate on the recognition of patterns that are relevant to several full-fledged diagnoses, without constituting a complete diagnosis in themselves.

The trellis architecture requires that we break our data-analysis problems into pieces of this sort; then we organize the pieces into a hierarchical graph, an "information flow" hierarchy that mirrors the *conceptual* hierarchy of the problem. Conceptually low-level processes are at the bottom of the graph, high-level processes at the top. We can connect the bottom level of processes directly to data sources in the outside world. Data flows into the program at the bottom, and percolates upwards.

All processes in the graph execute continuously and concurrently, and they communicate among themselves and with the outside world using a simple and uniform protocol. Each process can be regarded as driving a meter that displays, at all times, the current status of the sub-problem it's focussed on—the latest input value in some data stream, the probability that a given diagnosis correctly describes the situation, and so on. The parallelism in this architecture is important for two reasons. First, it will make it possible to apply lots of computational power to the problem—in many cases, the outputs of our analysis will be useless if they aren't available quickly. Second, it will allow us to build a clean, modular program out of conceptually-independent pieces.

Clearly, we've described a specialist-parallel problem. We noted in chapter 3 that *"specialist parallelism* involves programs that are conceived in terms of a logical network. They arise when an algorithm or a system to be modelled is best understood as a network in which each node executes a relatively autonomous computation, and inter-node communication follows predictable paths. The network may reflect a physical model, or the logical structure of an algorithm..."

The network in our case clearly reflects *logical* as opposed to physical problem structure.

In the following section we discuss the trellis architecture in greater detail, and a natural specialist-parallel approach. We go on to discuss refinements in the interest of efficiency—raising, in the final section, the important question of realtime execution. Realtime is a highly specialized topic that we can't discuss in detail, but we introduce several important points. Again, the real topic isn't the trellis architecture; it's the highly significant *type* of problem that the trellis represents.

The experiments with the trellis we discuss below were conducted by Michael Factor. His thesis [Fac90] is the definitive guide to this work.

8.3   The process trellis architecture

Each node in the trellis (where a node is simply a decision process)
continuously attempts to calculate a state based upon the states of inferior nodes. When sufficient information is available from a node's
inferiors—each decision process defines for itself what "sufficient information" means—it generates a new state. As a result, nodes one level
up may recalculate their own states, and so on.

We supply two types of "logic probe" with the system, "write probes"
and "read probes," in order to accomplish input and output. Write
probes are used to pump values into the system; read probes suck results
out.

Touching a node with a write probe allows us to set the state of that node
to any value we choose. If we squeeze the write probe's trigger (every
probe comes equipped with a trigger), we cause the node whose state
has just been reset to *recompute* its state. Touching a node with a read
probe causes the node's current state to be returned. This current state
can then be displayed somehow on a terminal connected to the program.
The node's current state might be unknown -- insufficient data. If
so, we can squeeze the read probe's trigger; this causes a *query* to be
sent to the node we are touching. When a node is queried, it attempts to
compute a new, current state. If it fails, it identifies which data values
it's missing—which of its inferiors, in other words, have failed to report
values that are required by its state-computing function. It then sends
queries downwards to each one of these inferior nodes.

The interface between the trellis and the human user is constructed using
probes; probes can also be used to wire separate trellises together into
a larger ensemble.

For concreteness, figure 8.1 shows a diagram representing the functions
of each level of a trellis for patient monitoring in an intensive care unit.
Figure 8.2 shows the complete structure of this program as it existed in
Fall 1989.

> *Massive parallelism:* One of the most interesting aspects of
> the trellis architecture is its inherent scalability. It's easy to
> conceive of applications for ten-thousand node trellises (and

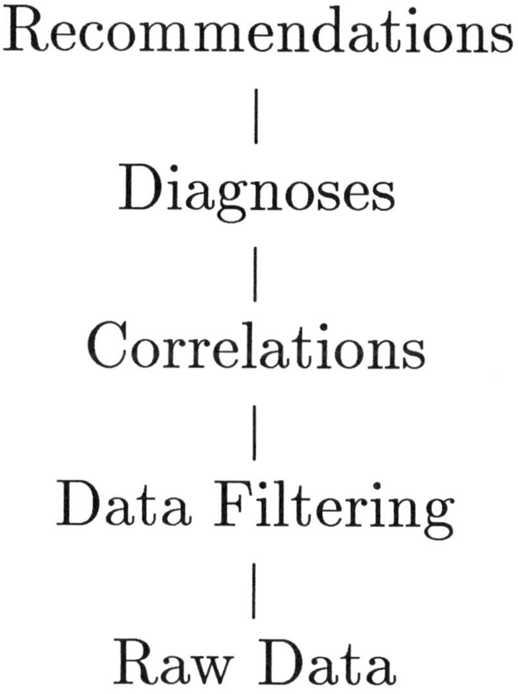

Recommendations

|

Diagnoses

|

Correlations

|

Data Filtering

|

Raw Data

Figure 8.1
The information-flow hierarchy of a trellis program for intensive care unit monitoring.

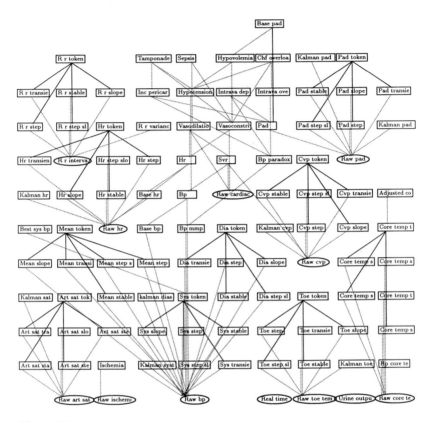

Figure 8.2
The trellis graph for an intensive care unit monitor. The node labels are obscure,
and the details (in any case) irrelevant to this discussion; but the graph should
make the general character of this application—how many levels it has, what kind
of interconnection patterns and dependence relations hold—clear enough. This
program represents joint work with Drs. Perry Miller, Dean Sittig and Aaron
Cohen of the Department of Anaesthesiology and the Medical Informatics Program
at the Yale Medical School.

beyond); and it's fairly easy to conceive of building such programs.

In very large trellises, many nodes will be similar or identical in structure. This is true, for example, of a current trellis design that focussed on a stock market in an attempt to detect insider trading; the design encompasses thousands of nodes, but many are identical in structure. A transportation network might have a large number of segments all of which must be monitored separately and continuously, but the logic required will be basically the same in all cases; hence we may have, say, a thousand separate segments, each involving an identical 10-node sub-trellis. The complete program, of course, would involve other differentiated nodes as well. Scientific data gathering (in astronomy or weather domains, for example) may involve hundreds of data sources, to most of which essentially the same set of trends-detection filtering nodes may be attached.

Of course, many trellis domains will require a large collection of separate and distinct nodes. Our medical collaborators estimate that the ICU trellis will incorporate several hundred nodes, most distinct in design, when it's finished; but this trellis focusses only on hemodynamic monitoring. A general-purpose trellis for monitoring intensive care patients in all areas might require thousands of distinct nodes. The trellis architecture and its development environment is designed with the future needs of very large programs specifically in mind.

This discussion omits some fairly significant details. But it's sufficient to allow us to study the programming methodology issues that the trellis raises.

8.4 The specialist parallel approach

The specialist-parallel implementation is natural and suggests itself immediately. Basically, our strategy will be to implement each node in the

trellis by a separate process. If our trellis has 100 nodes, we execute 100
`eval` operations to create 100 separate processes.

In this scheme of things, each process has the following structure:

```
while (TRUE)
    if ( any of my inferiors has transmitted a new state) {
        recompute my own state;
        if ( my state has changed)
            transmit the new state upwards to my superiors;
    }
    else if ( any of my superiors has transmitted a query) {
        try to recompute my state;
        if ( I succeed)
            transmit the new state upwards to my superiors;
        else
            transmit the query downwards to each inferior
            from whom I need more information;
    }
```

This outline ignores several points. First, it doesn't deal with probes;
they are handled in the same fashion as upward-filtering values (write
probes) or downward-filtering queries (read probes). If a node is top-
or bottom-level, a new state or query is (clearly) propagated no farther.
If a higher-level node appeals for data to the bottom level, and the
bottom level doesn't have any data, the buck stops there, so far as the
trellis itself is concerned. If a read-probe is attached to this bottom-level
node, though, the node's current status gets reported (via the probe) to
a display. It becomes the user's duty to supply the necessary data (via
write-probe).

There are two reasonable, closely-related strategies for implementing
this scheme.

First, we might provide one input stream for each node: in this case,
whether I have new data to pass *upwards* to node Q, or a query to pass
downwards to Q, I attach a tuple to Q's unique input stream. In this
case, each process will work roughly as shown in figure 8.3.

Each process's input stream is a multiple-source one-sink in-stream of
the sort discussed in chapter 3. Each node maintains a head index

```
while (TRUE) {
    get the next tuple from my input stream;
    if ( the tuple shows that one of my inferiors has
        transmitted a new state) {
            recompute my own state;
            if ( my state has changed)
                attach tuples recording my new state to
                the input streams of each superior;
    }
    else if ( the tuples shows that one of my superiors has
            transmitted a a query) {
        try to recompute my state;
        if ( I succeed)
            attach state tuples to superior streams;
    else
        attach query tuples to each inferior's
        stream from whom I need more information;
    }
}
```

Figure 8.3
Process outline for a specialist-parallel trellis.

locally; the tail index floats in a tuple. Accordingly, we implement

get the next tuple from my input stream

using a statement like

```
in("Q-stream", ++head, ?information);
```

information is probably a struct; one field of this struct indicates
whether this tuple holds a state or a query. To attach a tuple to R's
stream, we use a sequence like

```
in("R-stream tail", ?index);
out("R-stream tail", index+1);
out("R-stream", index, NewInformation);
```

The other strategy is (perhaps) slightly cleaner and more modular. We
implement each trellis node by means of *two* processes; one handles
upward-filtering data, the other downward-filtering queries. Node Q has
two streams associated with it, a query stream and a data stream. Each
of the two processes associated with Q reads one stream. Q's current
state is stored in tuple space, where each of the two processes can access
it. The query and data streams are each in-streams of exactly the sort
described above.

To complete the package, we need some computational routines to install
in our coordination framework. One way to understand the computation is in terms of a set of state-computing procedures, one for each
trellis node. A state-computing routine could accept a single struct
as an argument. The first component of the struct holds the previous
state of *this* node; the next components specify the current state of the
other nodes upon which this node's state depends. The state-computing
routine attempts to compute a new state, and if it succeeds, it assigns
the new state value to the first field of its argument struct, and returns
TRUE. If it can't compute a new state, because of insufficient data, it returns FALSE. In this case, it assigns to the last field of the struct a value
indicating *which* inferior nodes are responsible for the state-computing
failure—which nodes, in other words, must be queried for more data.

For concreteness, let's say that some node is intended to calculate the
likelihood that a patient is about to get a headache: when headache-
likelihood rises to the "highly probable" level, we can give the patient

some aspirin. Let's say that headache-likelihood depends on the state of three inferior nodes: the *fatigue* node, the *hungry* node, and the *arguing with flat-earth activists, unreconstructed Trotskyites or functional programmers* node. The headache-likelihood node also depends on its *own* previous state: even if all irritants suddenly disappear, a headache doesn't dissipate instantly.

We implement headache-likelihood by a routine that accepts a single five-field `struct`. The routine looks at the input `struct` and attempts to compute the current headache-likelihood. Suppose that the *currently arguing* node's state is FALSE, but that we have *no* current values for *fatigue* and *hungry* (their slots in the argument `struct` are filled by a NO-VALUE token). In this case, the headache node might decide that it has insufficient data to compute a new state. It assigns NO-VALUE to its own current state, assigns *headache* and *fatigue* to the last ("values needed") field of the argument STRUCT, and returns FALSE. (Note, on the other hand, that if *arguing* were TRUE, and had been true for—say—the last ten minutes, the headache node might well have decided that its current state was "*highly probable*" or even "*certain*" *despite* the lack of current data from the *fatigue* and the *hungry* nodes.)

Once we've specified each node's state function, we can build the co-ordination envelope that wraps around it. Suppose we are using the one-process-per-node coordination framework. Each node *f* has two corresponding routines: `f_state()` and `f_envelope()`. `f_state` implements *f*'s decision logic: it produces a new state given the appropriate input values. `f_envelope` handles inter-node communication, and invokes `f_state` as appropriate. See figure 8.4.

To create the trellis, we simply execute an

```
eval("Node f", f_envelope());
```

for every trellis node.

8.5   A specialist ⇒ agenda transformation

The main performance problem with our specialist-parallel starting-point is, again, *load balancing*.

```
void f_envelope()
{
  ...
struct {
  stateType MyState, FatigueState, HungryState,
ArguingState;
  Boolean ValuesNeeded[2];
  /* if ValuesNeeded[0] is TRUE, need a new
FatigueState... */
  } CURRENT;
while (TRUE) {
    get the next tuple from my input stream;
    if ( an inferior has sent a new state) {
        update field values of CURRENT;
        f_state(CURRENT);
        if ( CURRENT.MyState has changed)
            attach tuples recording my new state to
            the input streams of each superior;
    }
    else if ( a superior has sent a query) {
        if ( f_state(CURRENT) )
            /* recall f_state() yields TRUE if it succeeds */
            attach state tuples to superior streams;
        else
            attach query tuples to the streams
            of each node mentioned in CURRENT.ValuesNeeded;
    }
}
```

Figure 8.4
The process envelope for a specialist-parallel trellis.

If we're going to create one process for every node in a trellis, the result is (potentially) lots of processes. We might in principle execute the trellis on a parallel machine that has one processor for every trellis process, but that's unlikely. In most cases, it's also unnecessary and undesirable. In order to give adequate performance (to handle information fast enough to be useful), trellis programs will in general need to run on many processors simultaneously. But when each trellis node performs a relatively modest computation, it doesn't need a whole processor to itself; it can perfectly well share a processor with other trellis nodes. Thus we might have, say, a one-hundred node trellis (hence, let's say, a one-hundred process parallel program, in the specialist-parallel version) that executes too slowly on a single processor, but whose computational requirements can easily be met, in principle, by a five-processor parallel workstation.

Our problem in the latter case is again, in line with the previous chapter, to deploy one hundred processes onto five processors in a reasonable way. We can't simply dump twenty randomly-chosen processes onto each processor: unless every process does the same thing (recall that a trellis is specifically a *heterogeneous* process ensemble), some processors will wind up with a lot more work than other processors. As we've discussed, this kind of poor load balance is bad for performance. Performance is constrained by the speed of the slowest (*i.e.* the most heavily burdened) processor. And we've discussed the disadvantages in making assumptions about any automatic process-reshuffling capabilities that the runtime support system might have.

As an alternative, a software architecture like the trellis lends itself to some (fairly sophisticated) "static scheduling" techniques—techniques to assign work to processors in such a way that load is well-balanced at runtime. We discuss these techniques in the next section. Here we describe a simpler approach, which also lays the groundwork for the next variation.

We can use exactly the sort of abstraction transformation discussed in chapter 2 to transform our specialist- to an agenda-parallel solution, in the process solving our load-balance problem.

As discussed in chapter 2, abstraction requires that we "raise the processes one level in the conceptual scheme." In our case, each process will compute *many* trellis states on each iteration, rather than embodying a single trellis node. A node's current state will be represented by a state tuple. Hence a thousand-node trellis implies the existence of a thousand state-tuples in tuple space, *not* 1000 separate processes. The "agenda" is simple:

```
while (TRUE) {
    accept and install any new input data values
      or queries;
    update every node's state;
}
```

Clearly, the second agenda item entails many tasks; we can throw as many workers as we want (up to a maximum of one per trellis node) into the updating process. In other words, we'll do the following. We execute an unbounded series of iterations. On each iteration, we accept input (data or queries) from the outside world; then we send a collection of identical worker processes sweeping over the trellis. Each worker grabs a node-describing tuple, updates the corresponding node's state and repeats, until no more nodes remain to be updated. Then we go on to the next iteration.

We've solved our load-balancing problem: tasks are distributed dynamically to worker processes on each sweep. We no longer face the problem of allocating processes to processors: each processor executes a single worker process. Note also that under our new scheme, all trellis interconnection information is localized in the master process. Rewiring the trellis—adding or deleting a node, or changing decision procedures and, consequently, the interconnection pattern—require changes to a single table in the master process only.

In the implementation of this scheme, our basic data structure will be a task bag of the type discussed several times previously. This time, though, we need to implement an iterative bag structure—once every task in a given bag has been processed, workers must proceed to the next bag (or, alternatively, the single bag must be refilled with the next iteration's tasks).

There are (as usual) many ways to implement this scheme. We'll describe one simple version. We have a master and n worker processes. The master maintains a data structure that describes the current state of every node in the trellis. At the start of each iteration, the master accepts new data values and queries. Some nodes will have to be updated on this sweep and others won't. Nodes whose inferiors have changed state, whose superiors have sent them a query or who have been touched by a triggered probe will need to updated; others won't. The master creates one task-describing tuple for each node that requires updating, and dumps the tuples into a bag.

The master executes the following loop:

```
while (TRUE) {
    /* for the indefinite lifespan of this program */
    accept input values or queries;
    identify nodes that need to be updated this iteration;
    for ( each node that needs updating) {
        ++TasksThisRound;
        out("task", TaskDescription);
    };
    for (; TasksThisRound--; ) {
        in("result", ?NewStateValue);
        record NewStateValue;
    }
}
```

The worker's coordination framework is simple:

```
while (TRUE) {
    in("task", ?TaskDescription);
    compute a new state for this node;
    out("result", NewStateValue);
}
```

The computational part of the program is essentially the same as what we described in the previous section. A task in this agenda-parallel version corresponds to the arrival of a new input-stream tuple in the specialist-parallel program. The only significant difference is that, in this new version, state- and query- tuples aren't attached to the input streams of the relevant nodes. Instead, the fact that a new state has been computed or that a query must be propagated is simply recorded in the `NewStateValue` that is returned to the master in the result tuple. The master is responsible for updating the trellis data structure and scheduling the relevant nodes for execution during the next sweep.

Note that we've achieved not only dynamic load balancing but, as usual in our agenda-parallel schemes, control over granularity. If the update computation at a given node is too minor to cover the overhead of task-ing, the master process can group updates into clumps, dynamically if necessary.

Variants of the scheme are possible under which there is no master, merely a collection of identical workers. We discuss such a scheme in the exercises.

8.6   Static scheduling and realtime

Now we come to the hard part. Suppose that we require not merely that a trellis perform "well," but that it perform in *realtime*? Specifically: input values arrive from the external world at a certain maximum frequency. How can we guarantee that each new set of values is fully processed before the next crop arrives? That each new set of values entering at the bottom has percolated throughout the trellis before the next set is pumped in?

"Realtime" is a word that lacks a canonical definition. We don't require our program to meet so-called "hard realtime" constraints—it needn't deliver reliably predictable performance on a time scale that is comparable to a processor's clock frequency. Hard realtime performance would require a realtime operating system and a realtime Linda implementation. The operating system would have to avoid all sources of unpredictable runtime at any scale (virtual memory, for example). The Linda system would be required to report detailed expected-performance estimates for all Linda operations, based on the runtime data structures chosen by the optimizer for each tuple class. Having provided such a foundation, we could then implement a hard realtime system using the techniques we'll describe below. But the system we'll describe *does* meet the *relevant* realtime constraints for its domain without this added complexity. In the medical monitoring domain, we need to be able to guarantee performance on a time scale of seconds, not of microseconds. This kind of constraint is typical of many problems in the software-monitor domain.

Our agenda-parallel trellis implementation allows us to make certain statements that are germane to the realtime question. We know that, in the worst case, assimilating a completely new set of data values will require that every node in the trellis be updated. These updates will be distributed over a series of iterations—in the first iteration the bottom-level of nodes is updated, then the next level and so on. We know, too, how long it takes to update each node. The state-computing functions associated with each node are fixed, of course; we can simply time arbitrarily many executions of each node-update step and choose worst-case values. (Obviously, we must be able to guarantee that each state function behaves in a fairly predictable way and that it always converges. Our goal in general is the following: given a collection of well-behaved, predictable state functions, build a parallel program that is also well-behaved and predictable.)

Because we know the worst-case amount of work that is required in order to process a new set of input values, we can predict approximately how long a complete update of the trellis will require, given some number of workers among whom the tasks are being shared.

Unfortunately, though, the dynamic nature of task-assignment in our agenda-parallel program introduces some uncertainty into the timing: we don't know exactly which tasks each worker will grab, and so we can't predict exactly how long each iteration will take. Dynamic task-assignment introduces a measure of overhead as well as some uncertainty about timings. Dumping task tuples into tuple space, and removing them, takes time. If each worker knew *a priori* exactly what tasks it would be required to perform on each iteration, we wouldn't need to distribute task tuples.

Ordinarily we're happy to pay the costs of such a distribution, because arriving at a good static distribution of tasks would be difficult or impossible, and the costs of dynamic tasking are often small. But the realtime trellis case is different. The fixed structure of the trellis, and the predictable nature of trellis execution, make it possible to arrive at a good static schedule. Furthermore, when we are dealing with realtime requirements, predictability is crucial.

8.6.1   A realtime scheduling algorithm

The actual strategy followed in achieving realtime execution of the trellis
is complicated.   What is important here is the general flavor of the
approach.

First, we need to define exactly what we're trying to achieve.   If no
process generates a new state without receiving new information (either from an inferior or a write probe), any trellis program upon which
no probes are executed for a sufficiently long period of time eventually *stabilizes*—that is, reaches a state in which there are no enabled or
currently executing processes[1].   Under the iterative execution scheme,
any appropriately constrained trellis program stabilizes in no more than
$2\mathcal{H} + 1$ sweeps, where $\mathcal{H}$ is the height of the trellis (that is, the length of
the longest directed path).   For $\mathcal{H} + 1$ sweeps, states can flow upward to
the top of the trellis; for the next $\mathcal{H}$ sweeps, queries can flow downward
to the bottom of the trellis.   The stability property gives the trellis a
predictable, well-defined, worst-case behavior.

To make a real-time guarantee, we must know how frequently new data
values can arrive; we assume that the minimum interval that can pass
between the entry of a new set of data values is τ, the trellis's *period*.
Every τ seconds, one data value *or many values simultaneously* may
be entered.   We can now state our realtime execution requirement: the
program must run on enough processors so that it is guaranteed to be
able to analyze a set of inputs completely within its period, τ.   What does
it mean to "analyze a set of inputs completely?"   One obvious definition
is that the program must *stabilize* within τ.   Hence, we require that our
realtime execution scheme be able to complete $2\mathcal{H} + 1$ sweeps within τ
seconds.   Our goal is to find the smallest number of processors that can
meet this requirement, and to discover *how* they can meet it—how we
can map trellis nodes to processors in such a way that the trellis will
stabilize within τ seconds.

Our general approach will be as follows.   Starting with the set of all
trellis nodes, we distribute node-descriptions onto processors.   During a
sweep, each processor will update all trellis nodes that it holds locally;
then it will send information about the results of the sweep to other
processors, in preparation for the next sweep.

---

[1]Assuming all processes terminate whenever they execute.

Factor's heuristic scheduler [Fac90] is a technique for placing node-descriptions onto processors in a way that's likely to use a minimal number of processors in meeting the goal—namely, trellis stabilization within τ seconds. ("Likely" because this is a scheduling *heuristic*; the scheduling problem can be shown to be NP-complete, thus not amenable to a provably optimal scheduling algorithm. As a trellis grows in size, such an algorithm would tend to run so slowly as to be useless.)

In order to perform this static assignment of trellis nodes to processors, we need an analytic model that allows us to predict how long it takes to execute a trellis until it stabilizes. We need such a model because our general procedure will be to assign trellis nodes incrementally to processors, evaluating at each stage how much time would be required to achieve stabilization given the configuration that exists so far. The analytic model will be expressed in terms of a collection of well-defined costs, most significantly the cost required to read a tuple from tuple space, to update a tuple (by removing and then re-inserting it), and to execute each node's update routine. We can then express the time required for a trellis to stabilize in terms of a combination of these costs, given a particular number of processors and some assignment of trellis nodes to processors.

Once we have a way of evaluating execution time given an assignment of trellis nodes to processors, we can execute the heuristic scheduling algorithm. The algorithm starts by assuming some fixed number of processors; then it tries to map trellis nodes onto those processors in such a way that the timing goal is achieved. If it fails, number-of-processors is incremented, and the procedure repeats.

Figure 8.5 gives some speedup results for several trellis programs running under the scheduler we've described.

8.7 Conclusions

The fact that we *can* design and assemble diverse, complex and potentially enormous parallel applications is reassuring. The fact that (having done so) we can make accurate predictions about their performance is remarkable. Parallel programming is a workable, practical, manageable reality.

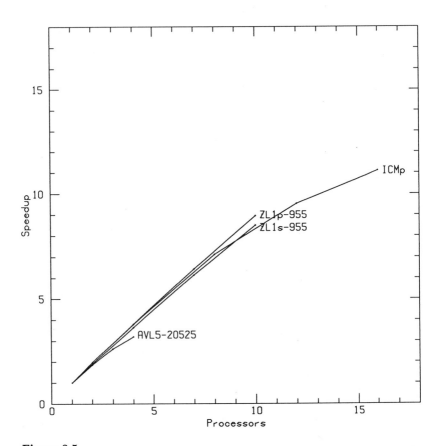

Figure 8.5
Speedup curves for several different trellis programs, running on shared-memory
multiprocessors. The sequential program for comparison purposes consists (in each
case) of an identical trellis program running on a single node and making no use of
tuple space. What's important to the trellis program is predictable performance
(stabilization within the required time-period) under *worst-case* conditions—not
optimal efficiency. The speedup figures graphed here don't represent linear
speedup, but they represent good performance given these problem requirements.
The curve labelled ICMp is the intensive care unit monitor we've discussed; the
curves labelled ZL1p and ZL1s are large, synthetic trellis programs (955 trellis nodes
each) running under two slightly different stabilization criteria. The curve labelled
AVL5 is a 20,525-node synthetic trellis. The synthetic trellises have "empty"
decision procedures (they merely loop, killing time) and random connectivity; they
allow us to study the behavior of this software architecture for very large programs.

Among problems that lend themselves to network-shaped solutions, **circuit simulation** is one of the most interesting. It requires that we step a circuit through a series of iterations as we trace signals and record the circuit's behavior. Such problems tend to be highly compute-intensive and highly parallelizable. **Neural network** emulators are another example. Many **graph problems** lend themselves to programming in this style; we discuss one simple example in the exercises.

8.8 Exercises

Preliminary. The first three questions ask you to build trellis programs of various kinds. First, though, we need to address the obvious preliminary question: a trellis program that does *what?* To build a complete trellis, you need a hierarchical understanding of some domain, and a set of decision procedures in which this understanding is captured precisely. (In the experiments we've conducted, we built the coordination framework but other people supplied the domain expertise.)

These questions don't assume a fixed size trellis, but you should assemble roughly 50 decision procedures at least (arranged, perhaps, in 5 levels) in order to attack them seriously. There are three reasonable ways to get these decision procedures; we'll list them in order, from less to more interesting.

First, you could use synthetic decision procedures that do nothing: they read inferior-node states (which you can assume are arbitrary integers), spin in a loop for some number of iterations to kill time, and then generate their own new, arbitrary "state." (This kind of synthetic trellis is actually very useful for performance experiments, because it can be parameterized. You can test many different sorts of trellises by varying the height-*vs.*-width of the trellis, the average number of inferior states each state depends on, and the average granularity of the decision procedures.)

Second, you can make up your own set of decision procedures. Choose an arbitrary domain (or one you find interesting), and improvise something. (We carried out initial trellis experiments in this way, targeted at automobile traffic networks. The point was to infer the location of traffic blockages, and to reprogram traffic lights and highway-entrance-control lights dynamically for better throughput.)

Third, you can find a real domain expert. Most universities employ a fair number of such people. Rumor has it that domain expertise can sometimes be found in the non-academic world as well. You might talk to medical people, to experts on finance, markets or economics generally, to people with knowledge of factories, or of multi-factory manufacturing structures, to networks people (at telephone companies, for example), to experts on any kind of transportation system, to scientists (particularly physicists) with large experimental setups to monitor, and so on. The potential applicability of powerful expert monitors is nearly unlimited.

1. Build a specialist-parallel trellis of the sort described in section 2; then build an agenda-parallel version of the master-worker variety discussed in section 3. Compare the expressivity and efficiency of the two versions.

Suppose that your trellis problem were *non*-compute intensive: the computing power of a single processor is ample to run it effectively. Is the trellis nonetheless a good software architecture for the monitoring problem? Which implementation strategy is better in this case—specialist or agenda?

2. The master process in the agenda-parallel trellis you've just built is a potential bottleneck for large trellises. Build a new version that supports multiple master processes (run your version with three masters, let's say, for concreteness). Clearly, workers should be able to grab tasks generated by any master. There are (at least) two possible ways to handle the result tuples. They might be sent not to *any* master but to the right one; masters under this scheme may need to exchange some information, so that they are aware of state information describing trellis nodes that are adjacent to any nodes they own. Or, every master might read *each* result tuple, updating its own part of the trellis graph as appropriate. If you use this second scheme, you should implement a "garbage collected" read stream—result tuples are removed from the read stream once all master processes have seen them.

3. Another way to deal with the master-as-bottleneck problem is to eliminate the master altogether. Modify your trellis program to make all processes worker processes.

4. **Graph algorithms** of various kinds can be programmed using the techniques discussed in this chapter. Developing a cost-ordered list of all paths between two nodes in a graph is a simple example. Write such a program using the "bug trudger" algorithm: create a bug and place it on the origin node. Arrange for the bug to trudge outwards through the graph, generating new bugs whenever more than one path is available. Each bug remembers the path it's taken so far. The destination node welcomes each incoming bug, squashes it, retrieves the information it contains and inserts this data in a cost-ordered list. You must make sure, of course, that bugs don't wander in circles.

Program this algorithm either in specialist or in agenda style.

☐ (*Turingware:*) 5. Human organizations are generally arranged in tree-form: each person has a unique boss and (potentially) many boss-ees. What are the implications of arranging a human organization as a "person trellis"?—each individual has a place in a trellis graph; this trellis represents the information-flow hierarchy within the organization. Hence, each individual has, potentially, many semi-bosses and semi-boss-ees. Are there organizations for which such a strategy might be appropriate? What is the role of read and write probes in such a structure? Would a (software) process trellis be a useful inter-person communication device in such an environment? Are there any uses for a mixed process-person trellis, in which some trellis nodes are processes and others are people? (To put these questions in another way: would it be possible to make all interactions with such an organization systematic, all mediated by the same software support tools? Might inquiries from outside the organization be "attached" automatically to the right trellis node? Might many sub-organizations be coordinated systematically, using probes, into a single multi-trellis? Might directors or accountants or investors monitor such an organization by attaching probes as needed? Might *any* employee get the opportunity to take in the "big picture" by attaching his own probes?)

9 Coordinated Programming

9.1 And now for something completely different

We noted in the introduction that our topic in the broader sense was *coordinated programming*. We can use the term *coordination* to refer to the process of *building programs by gluing together active pieces*. Each "active piece" is a process, task, thread or any other locus of execution independent of (and asynchronous with) the rest. *Gluing active pieces together* means gathering them into an ensemble in such a way that we can regard the ensemble itself as the program. The gluing process requires that we allow independent activities to communicate and to synchronize with each other exactly as they need to. This definition is vague and broad, which is the whole point.

Parallel programming is one important sub-topic within this general category. But as we noted, many other program types fall into the "coordination" class as well. *Distributed systems,* which use many processes because they encompass many separate and autonomous computers, are coordinated programs. The term *concurrent system* is sometimes used in the special sense of a multi-process program running on a single processor. (Operating systems for conventional machines are often concurrent systems; they use multiple processes in the interests of a clean and simple software structure, and to support user-level time-sharing or multi-programming.) Concurrent systems are clearly *coordinated* systems as well. *Time-coordinated systems* are coordinated programs; mixed-language programs may qualify as well.

We can't cover this entire ground in one chapter. We focus on a single problem that is simultaneously a *distributed system,* a *concurrent operating system* and a *time-coordinated system* problem. We prepare for this discussion by considering two "classical problems" in coordinated programming, *dining philosophers* and the *readers-writers problem*. Neither problem is terribly important in itself, but they both deal in an abstract way with issues that are typical of this broader class of applications.

Note that concurrency *is already intrinsic* to the applications we discuss in this chapter. We don't have to decide where to put it; we merely need to figure out how to deal with it—how to glue a bunch of concurrent activities into a satisfactory ensemble.

9.1.1   Two classical problems

The "dining philosophers" problem goes like this: a round table is set with some number of plates (traditionally five); there's a single chopstick between each two plates, and a bowl of rice in the center of the table. Philosophers think, then enter the room, eat, leave the room and repeat the cycle. A philosopher can't eat without two chopsticks in hand; the two he needs are the ones to the left and the right of the plate at which he is seated. If the table is full and all philosophers simultaneously grab their left chopsticks, no right chopsticks are available and deadlock ensues. To prevent deadlock, we allow only four philosophers (or one less than the total number of plates) into the room at any one time.

The dining philosophers problem was posed originally by Dijkstra, and has long been used to test the expressivity of new concurrent, parallel or coordination languages[1].

The software problem in this scenario is the following: write a program that has five concurrent processes (the philosophers) and five "resources" (the chopsticks). Each process executes an infinite loop in which it is guaranteed, at regular intervals, to need a particular set of two resources from among the five. The ensemble must be put together in such a way

---

[1] In older discussions of the problem, for example Hoare's treatment in his "Concurrent Sequential Processes [Hoa78]," there was a bowl of spaghetti in the center of the table and a *fork* between every two plates. But the problem in this form was simply too hard for the average computer science student, who was rarely able to figure out why a philosopher or anyone else shouldn't be able to make do with one fork in a pinch. In a seminal contribution, Ringwood [Rin88] realized that, although a single fork is in most cases perfectly serviceable, a single chopstick is another matter. We use Ringwood's version here, but of course this still leaves several questions unanswered—why, for example, philosophers are such unsanitary people that they're willing to grab someone else's chopstick and chow down without a second thought, and whether it's really fair to assume that the typical philosopher knows how to eat rice with *any* number of chopsticks. And of course, even the new and improved formulation leaves the functional programmers still trying to figure out how you can eat rice without actually consuming any of it. In any case, further development of the problem statement should be regarded as an exercise. Mail your contributions to Professor Ringwood in London.

that each a process gets the resources it needs eventually—no process or group of processes ever gets stuck and waits indefinitely.

Dining philosophers is an abstraction of problems that arise when concurrent processes contend for a fixed collection of resources. The resources might be access to protected parts of the operating system, to devices, or to arbitrary shared data objects. In the problem to be discussed in the next section, for example, concurrent processes contend for access to a set of objects representing appointment calendars.

9.1.2 A solution

There are Num philosophers in total; we'll only let Num - 1 of them into the dining room at the same time. If were to allow all Num philosophers to be in the room at the same time, it becomes possible for all philosophers to grab their left chopsticks simultaneously, and then—deadlock. No philosopher can eat, because none has more than one chopstick. No philosopher will relinquish a chopstick: you are not allowed to put down your chopsticks until you are done eating. With no more than Num - 1 philosophers in the room, on the other hand, there's guaranteed to be at least *one* philosopher who is able to make use both of his left and of his right chopstick.

(We can show that this is true by using a simple combinatorial argument based on the pigeonhole principle. Consider $n - 1$ bins and n balls. In every distribution of the n balls among the $n - 1$ bins, there must be at least one bin that winds up holding at least two balls. Now if we associate each bin with a philosopher and each ball with a chopstick, it's clear that the set of all legal distributions of chopsticks to philosophers is a subset of the possible distributions of balls into bins—a chopstick can be grabbed only by the fellow on its right or on its left, and hence the corresponding ball can only land in one of the corresponding two bins. Since every distribution in the original set must assign two balls to one bin, it follows that every distribution in any *subset* of the original set must also assign two balls to one bin, and we conclude that at least one philosopher will be guaranteed to succeed in grabbing two chopsticks.)

So long as one philosopher can eat, deadlock is impossible. When the eating philosopher is done, he puts his chopsticks down, and they become available to the philosophers to his left and right. (In principle, a philosopher could put down his chopsticks, leave the room, then race back in again and grab both chopsticks before either of his stunned colleagues has made a move. We will return to this possibility.)

A solution to the problem now becomes straightforward (figure 1). We'll allow only Num - 1 philosophers into the room at a time; to accomplish this, we create Num - 1 "tickets" and set them adrift in tuple space. We require a philosopher to grab a ticket (using in) before he enters the room and starts contending for chopsticks, and to release his ticket (using out) when he's done eating and ready to leave. Each chopstick is represented by a tuple; philosophers grab chopsticks using in and release them using out.

To return now to the speedy philosopher problem: careful readers will notice that, if the Linda implementation is "unfair"—if it can repeatedly bypass one process blocked on in in favor of others—the Linda solution allows indefinite overtaking or livelock. A slow philosopher could remain blocked on an in("room ticket") statement while a speedy one repeatedly outs a room ticket and then grabs it again, leaving the slow philosopher still blocked; likewise with respect to the in("chopstick", ...) operation. We need to assume, then, that our Linda systems are "fair," which is a common assumption in dealing with non-deterministic programming environments. We must assume that, if matching tuples are available, a process blocked on in or rd will eventually have a matching tuple delivered to it. It will *not* be indefinitely bypassed while other blocked processes are continued.

9.1.3   The readers/writers problem

Suppose many processes share access to a complex data object (which is too large, we assume, to be conveniently stored in a single Linda tuple). Processes are permitted direct access to the shared object, but only after they get permission to do so. The rules of access specify that many readers or a single writer may have access to the object, but not both; a constant stream of read-requests must furthermore not be allowed to postpone satisfaction of a write request indef-

```
phil(i)
   int i;
{
   while(1) {
    think();
    in("room ticket");
    in("chopstick", i);
    in("chopstick", (i+1)%Num);
    eat();
    out("chopstick", i);
    out("chopstick", (i+1)%Num);
    out("room ticket");
   }
}

initialize()
{
   int i;
   for (i = 0; i < Num; i++) {
    out("chopstick", i);
    eval(phil(i));
    if (i < (Num-1)) out("room ticket");
   }
}
```

Figure 9.1
Dining philosophers.

initely, nor may a stream of write-requests indefinitely postpone reading.

The simplest and clearest way to solve this problem is to append each new read or write request to the end of a single queue. If the queue's head request is a read request, the requestor is permitted to proceed as soon as no writer is active; if the head request is a write request, it is permitted to proceed as soon as neither readers nor a writer are active. When a reader or writer is given permission to proceed, its request is removed from the head of the queue; the requesting process reads or writes directly, and notifies the system when it is done.

Reader processes will execute

```
startread();
  read;
stopread();
```

and writers similarly. All readers and writers determine on their own when it is permissible to proceed. They do so by manipulating four shared counters. When a process needs to read or write, it consults (and increments) the value of the rw-tail counter. Suppose the value of this counter was j. The request process now waits until the value of the rw-head counter is j: when it is, this requestor is first on line and will be the next process to be permitted access to the shared object. Before proceeding, though, it must wait for the value of the active-writers counter to be 0—when and only when this counter is 0, no writers have access to the shared object. If the requesting process is *itself* a writer, it must also wait for the active-readers counter to be 0. (Readers can share access with other readers, but writers share access with nobody.) Finally, the requestor increments either active-writers or active-readers (depending on whether it intends to write or read), and increments the rw-head counter to give the next waiting process a chance to await access at the head of the line.

startread()—the routine that is executed as a preface to reading—is

```
startread()
{
  rd("rw-head", incr("rw-tail"));
```

```
    rd("writers", 0);
    incr("active-readers");
    incr("rw-head");
}
```

incr is a routine that increments a shared counter stored in a tuple, ining the tuple, outing it after incrementing an integer count field, and returning the former (that is, the unincremented) value of the integer counter:

```
int incr(CounterName);
...
{
    ...
    in(CounterName, ?value);
    out(CounterName, value + 1);
    return value;
}
```

> *Pop Quiz:* we've outlined the basics; complete the implementation of the readers-writers system.

9.2   The meeting maker

As our main example in this chapter we'll use an exercise rather than a real system. All the code we discuss can be built and executed (see the exercises), but the result would be a demonstration or a prototype, not something that could be handed to users and put into service. A genuinely usable version of the system we'll discuss would require some important facilities, having to do with persistent storage and security, that are part of the Linda model conceptually but aren't supported by most current implementations.

Why study a prototype? First, this problem beautifully encapsulates exactly the range of issues that distinguish "coordinated" programs in general from parallel applications specifically. Second, the prototype's basic routines and data structures—its software architecture—are exactly what the real version would use. Studying the software architecture of the prototype exposes you to exactly the same logical issues as a real system would raise. Third, the sort of application we discuss here is becoming increasingly important. Linda implementations will soon provide the full complement of necessary features (some research implementations already address these issues). Other programming languages—in particular, ones that are intended specifically for distributed systems and not for parallel applications—already support the construction of this kind of system. In short, the topic is important, we can explore its logical ramifications in the context of a prototype, and support for real implementations isn't far behind.

9.2.1 The problem

Consider an organization in which each user has a workstation and all workstations are networked together—a standard, widespread environment. Occasionally the people in this organization need to meet with each other. Everybody maintains a calendar listing the periods of time during which he's generally willing to have meetings, as well as his current appointments.

We need to provide a package of routines that schedule meetings automatically *and* allow the participants in such meetings to discuss them beforehand. In general terms, then, our software package will address two major issues. First, scheduling meetings is a nuisance, and it ought to be automated if it can be. On the other hand, people generally don't like being handed edicts (especially by computers) to the effect that they *will* present themselves at such-and-such a place and time. Automatic meeting-scheduling is a potentially significant convenience, but *only* if the participants have an opportunity to ask questions, make comments and bow out if need be. Of course, the conversation as well as the scheduling should be software-supported.

A software-mediated conversation might give up a little something in charm and spontaneity to the old-fashioned variety (in which people actually gather around and talk to each other). On the other hand, it should also abolish the spatial and temporal barriers that constrain ordinary conversations. The participants in a software conversation don't need to share one place or one time. Users of electronic bulletin boards are familiar with the advantages of such free-floating electronic exchanges. What we need for our appointment-maker is something like an electronic bulletin board for every meeting—except that, in cases where all participants are logged on and joining in simultaneously, each person's comments should be made known to the others immediately. The result should be a sort of "real time" bulletin board that can function as a regular "archival" bulletin board as well.

To make the requirements precise, we'll trace through an example interaction with the system. We'll assume a multi-window display environment.

Let's say that Robert wants to schedule a half-hour meeting with Clara and Felix between 9 and 11 tomorrow. He types his request in the **try to schedule** window.

The system consults Clara's and Felix's calendars; let's say they're both available at 9:30. All three calendars are updated accordingly. A new message appears in the "calendar changes" window on all three displays, alerting Robert, Clara and Felix to the fact that they are scheduled to meet tomorrow at 9:30. A "conversation stream" is created, and each participant is invited to type comments in the **comments?** window.

Say Felix comments **what about?**; Robert replies **the new manual.** Felix then comments **forget it, I'm not coming. But meet with Clara.**

The schedule is changed accordingly. Clara, let's say, is not logged on; she hasn't participated in the conversation. Three hours later she shows up. She notes the change to her calendar and reads the associated conversation; then she adds a comment of her own (**OK, I'll be there**).

The "conversation stream" will continue to exist until the time of the meeting. When the participants are actively, simultaneously taking part, each one's comments should be passed on to the rest immediately. But the conversation stream should also support communication between participants whose contributions take place at separate time. The problem, in other words, has both "space-coordination" and "time-coordination" aspects.

9.2.2   The general form of a solution

Each user's calendar is stored in a tuple. A calendar can be read, then, by means of a simple rd operation; to be updated, the old calendar must be ined and the updated version outed.

A calendar tuple must include one field that identifies its owner, and a linear ordering must exist over these identification fields. If the identification fields are simply names (assuming everyone has a unique name), we can use alphabetical order; or they might be integer-valued "employee identification numbers," or whatever. The ordering is important when some user needs to consult and update many calendars in the course of scheduling a meeting. Calendars will always be ined in some fixed order, say lowest-to-highest, in order to eliminate the possibility of deadlocks.

(Why do we worry about deadlock? Suppose that Robert and Clara are simultaneously trying to schedule a meeting involving both of them. Robert grabs his calendar tuple and Clara grabs hers; then Robert tries to in Clara's and Clara to grab Robert's. Both ins block, and we have deadlock. Under an alphabetical ordering, on the other hand, Clara and Robert will both try to in Clara's calendar first. Whoever succeeds will find Robert's calendar available—assuming that no-one else is also trying to schedule a meeting.)

> *Pop Quiz:* prove that ining tuples under some fixed ordering, as described above, in fact prevents deadlock. Consider the conditions under which a cycle could arise in the resource graph that defines the problem. (For a discussion of resource graphs and deadlock, see Tanenbaum [Tan87, p. 124].)

We'll use *daemon processes* to alert users that their calendars have been changed. A daemon process is, in general, a process that waits for some condition to be true, takes some appropriate action in consequence, and repeats. (The awaited condition may be that n seconds have passed since this daemon last woke up. Operating systems often use daemons of this sort—a daemon process may wake up every now and then and flush the file buffers to disk, say, or recompute process priorities.) In our case, each user will have a daemon process that waits for his calendar tuple to be changed. When a scheduling process changes a calendar, the calendar tuple is replaced with a "Just Changed" flag raised in one of its fields. The appropriate daemon wakes up, removes the tuple, resets the "Just Changed" flag, replaces the tuple, and takes some appropriate action (for example, it prints a message in the "Calendar Changes" window).

The conversation streams are merely multi-source, multi-sink read-streams of the kind discussed in chapter 3. Each tuple in the stream holds a string representing a single comment. If a user of the system is logged on when his calendar changes, we can create a "listener" daemon for him and attach it to the conversation stream that will be associated with the newly-scheduled meeting. The listener daemon rds (and prints to the appropriate window) each newly-appended tuple in the conversation stream. When a user logs on much later, we can do exactly the same thing—create a listener daemon to read and print each comment in a conversation that actually took place much earlier.

9.2.3 Implementing the system.

We'll discuss the basic structure of each of the main routines in the appointment-maker. In every case, the code we'll present follows immediately from the description given.

First, consider the routine SetUpMeeting. It accepts as arguments a list of participants, a meeting-duration and the interval of time within which the meeting should take place. If it can schedule the meeting as requested, it goes ahead and does so; otherwise it returns failure, and the user tries again. (Obviously we might want SetUpMeeting to return, in the event of failure, the *reason* a meeting couldn't be scheduled—*e.g.* "Doris isn't available until noon." This and many other features are easy to provide. Here, though, we're concerned only with the basic coordination framework.)

A calendar tuple will take the following form:

```
("calendar", id, theCalendar, modified)
```

id identifies the calendar's owner; theCalendar represents times-available and meetings scheduled (probably in the form of an array or a struct); modified is set to TRUE whenever theCalendar is changed.

Suppose SetUpMeeting has been told to schedule a meeting whose participants are A, B and C. A, B and C might be names or some other identifiers; we'll assume that $A < B < C$ in the identifier ordering. In outline, SetUpMeeting will execute

```
in("calendar", A, ?Calendars[A], ?modified);
in("calendar", B, ?Calendars[B], ?modified);
in("calendar", C, ?Calendars[C], ?modified);
attempt to set up the requested meeting;
if ( the attempt succeeds) {
    assign this meeting a number that
        is unique over all meetings pending throughout the system;
    alter each participant's calendar to reflect the
        new meeting;
    out("calendar", A, Calendars[A], TRUE);
    out("calendar", B, Calendars[B], TRUE);
    out("calendar", C, Calendars[C], TRUE);
} else
    replace the calendar tuples without altering them;
```

When an attempt to schedule a meeting has succeeded, the meeting's initiator is responsible for setting up the associated conversation stream. The SetUpConvStream routine merely executes

```
out("conversation stream tail", MNUM, 1);
```

where MNUM is the new meeting's unique identifier.

Users want to be notified when their calendars have been changed. To accomplish this, they'll create a daemon that executes the routine MonitorCalendar, in outline

```
while (TRUE) {
    in("calendar", me, ?theNewCalendar, TRUE);
    out("calendar", me, theNewCalendar, FALSE);
    compare theNewCalendar to the old calendar and
        figure out what's changed;
    print an appropriate notice to the Calendar Changes window;
    for every new meeting on the calendar, create
        a Listener daemon;
}
```

The variable **me** is a formal parameter of the **MonitorCalendar** procedure; it identifies the user on whose behalf the daemon is working. To create the daemon, we use

```
eval("Monitor Calendar Daemon", MonitorCalendar(MyId));
```

Note that **MonitorCalendar** can't assume that only a *single* new meeting has appeared on the calendar. When a calendar tuple with its last field set to **TRUE** is dropped into tuple space, it's possible that another process intent on scheduling more meetings may grab it before **MonitorCalendar** does. We might also be operating in a setting in which a user's daemons are destroyed when he logs off. In this case, a newly fired-up **MonitorCalendar** may need to report a whole series of new meetings.

We turn now to the listener daemon. It executes a routine that scans a read-stream, checking each comment for a shut-down message.

We assume that the initiator of a meeting has the responsibility, once the scheduled hour has arrived, to append this "shut down" message to the associated conversation stream. We won't discuss this aspect of the problem further here, except to note that the process of appending shut-down messages can of course be automated—see the exercises. Appending a "shut down" to a comment stream has the effect of causing any daemons scanning the stream to terminate. No further comments will be printed automatically to user displays. But it's important to note that the conversation stream *itself* is *not* destroyed. It continues to exist; it may be scanned at any time by any interested party. In other words, conversations that precede meetings are part of the system's archives—they persist indefinitely in tuple space—until someone decides to destroy them.

The listener daemon executes the following routine (in outline):

```
void ListenTo(MtngNum); int MtngNum;
{
    ...
```

```
while (TRUE) {
  rd("conversation stream", MtngNum, ++i, ?comment);
  if ( the comment is "shut down") return;
  else  print the message in the appropriate window;
 }
}
```

To create a daemon to monitor a new conversation whose identifier is
MNUM, each user executes

```
eval("ListenerDaemon", ListenTo(MNUM));
```

Participants in the conversation must be able to comment as well as to
listen. The last of our basic routines allows users to comment, by installing a new tuple at the end of the appropriate conversation stream.
The routine MakeAComment accepts the meeting number and the comment (in the form of a character string) as arguments:

```
void MakeAComment(MNUM, TheComment);
int MNUM; char *TheComment;
{
  int index;
  in("conversation stream tail", MNUM, ?index);
  out("conversation stream tail", MNUM, index + 1);
  out("conversation stream", MNUM, index, TheComment);
}
```

Note that, if many participants try to comment simultaneously, their
comments are appended to the stream in some arbitrary order determined by the sequence in which they succeed in grabbing the
"conversation stream tail" tuple.

9.2.4 Characteristics of the solution: distribution, paral-
lelism, concurrency and time-coordination

How can we characterize our solution in general? Why is this example
significant?

First, we've designed a *distributed system* both in the physical and in
the logical sense. In the simple physical sense, a distributed system

runs in a host environment consisting of physically-dispersed machines. We've assumed for this exercise that each user has his own workstation. (As we noted in the first chapter, Linda has been implemented on local networks, and so our contention that we've been designing software for a distributed environment makes sense in practical terms.) A *logically* distributed system goes beyond mere physical distribution: it allows the *logic* of the system, the decision making, to be *shared* among participating machines, not centralized on one. In the system we've described there is a function called `SetUpMeeting`, and any user who wants to set up a meeting can execute this function *directly*, on his own machine. (He needn't send a message to some particular machine charged with scheduling everybody's meetings.) If eight different meetings are being organized, then eight different machines must be executing their local copies of the `SetUpMeeting` routine. Likewise, when a user needs to listen or add to a conversation stream, he executes the necessary code on his own machine.

Logically-distributed systems are interesting for several reasons. They avoid channelling activity through the potential bottleneck of a single machine. They expand gracefully: adding more users to the system probably means that more meetings will get scheduled, but does *not* necessarily mean that the load on any one machine will increase; each new machine on the network shares in the execution of the meeting-maker system. And logically-distributed systems *may* be more reliable—less prone to disruption when machines fail—than undistributed systems. (In our case, though, the reliability of the system we described depends on the reliability of the underlying Linda system. We can't make assumptions about the *system's* (*i.e. Linda's*) reliability on the basis of a particular *application's* being logically distributed.)

Logical distribution is related to another important characteristic of our example, hinted at above: it is a *parallel* program as well as a distributed one. It can make use of concurrency not only to accommodate the fact of physical distribution, but to improve performance. Suppose that, in a ten-user system, two users are trying to schedule new meetings and the other eight are split into two groups of four, each group conversing about an upcoming already-scheduled meeting. All ten workstations can be active simultaneously. As a system gets larger, and it becomes increasingly likely that many users will be planning meetings simultaneously, it's fair to expect that parallelism will make an increasingly significant contribution to good system performance (assuming, of course, that the underlying Linda system is well implemented).

Our meeting-maker is *concurrent* as well, in the special sense discussed previously: using multiple processes on a *single* processor in the interests of clean program structure.

When a user creates daemons, the daemon processes execute on his workstation, sharing its processor among themselves and all the other processes that this user may have started. When a single processor is shared among many processes—for example, among a "monitor calendar" daemon, several "listener" daemons and another process executing a command interpreter—we gain nothing in terms of execution speed. Five processes running on a single machine give us no better performance (in fact are guaranteed to give us slightly worse performance) than a single process carrying out all five functions by itself. But this kind of concurrency may be important, as it is here, because it supports clean program structure. The daemon idea, and the concurrent-process concept behind it, make it easy to design the "monitor calendar" and the "listener" routines. These ideas lead, too, to a system that naturally and dynamically adapts to a complex environment. In the system we designed, a single user might be involved in three different conversations simultaneously. No change or addition to the code is necessary to support this possibility—it happens automatically when the need arises.

Finally, the system we've designed is *time-coordinated* as well as space-coordinated, as we've discussed above. n users may participate in planning some meeting—one initiating it and all n entering into the associated conversation—despite the fact that no more than one of them is ever logged on at any given time.

In short, this example exercises virtually the entire armamentarium of multi-process programming. It is significantly more general in its demands than the parallelism examples that most of the book centers on; and it is a good representative of the "coordinated software" *genre* that, we've argued, can only grow steadily in significance.

> *Massive parallelism:* Large organizations may own thousands
> or tens of thousands of computers, usually interconnected in

some way. Electronic mail and file transfer services are generally available over large, far-flung networks, but highly-integrated services like the meeting maker usually are not. They certainly *will* be in the future, though. A ten-thousand person organization is *itself* a "massively parallel" system; if we give each worker a computer, and connect the computers together, massive parallelism inevitably follows. The meeting maker is in this sense one paradigm for an important class of massively parallel systems. If the underlying implementation is sound, it should be capable of scaling to enormous sizes.

We close by underlining those aspects of the exercise that require systems support beyond what most current Linda systems can supply. *Persistent tuple spaces* are this exercise's most crucial requirement. The fact that tuples persist indefinitely is part of Linda's semantics, but in most current systems a tuple space is destroyed when all the processes it contains have terminated. *Security* is vital: we can't allow unauthorized tampering with the tuples that define this application (can't allow, for example, one user to make arbitrary changes to another's calendar). This application must run in *system* or *privileged* mode, and make use of a *priviledged* tuple space—one that is accessible only to system-level routines of the sort we've described, not to arbitrary user-level code. Most current Linda systems don't support priviledged modes. Clearly *reliability* is another important issue: tuple space must be implemented in such a way that important tuples are unlikely to get lost even when machines fail. Persistent, secure and reliable implementations are fully consistent with Linda's semantics—to the programmer, in other words, they'll look essentially the same as any current Linda system looks—but they require implementation-level support. The necessary support is a major topic of research in our own group and in others.

9.3 Exercises

1. Implement the meeting-maker. (The main routines are outlined above, but the details and the overall framework are, of course, missing.)

If you're using a simulator running on a single processor, test the system by creating several concurrent "users" on your single processor—three is a reasonable number. We will name these users "1", "2", and "3" (after which, having strained our creative faculties to the limit, we will retire to the sofa for a short nap).

To avoid dealing with the creation and maintenance of lots of windows, implement one input and one output process. The input process accepts single-line commands like

```
1: schedule on Tues, betw 9 11, duration 0.5, with 3
```

and

```
3: comment meeting 3401, "what for?"
```

The prefixes (1: or 3:) identify which user is supposed to be doing the typing—*i.e.*, user 1 asks that a meeting be scheduled with user 3; user 3 comments on the meeting. (The input syntax doesn't have to be exactly like this; you can use anything that does the job.) The input process interprets these commands and invokes the appropriate routines.

The output process repeatedly withdraws tuples from the head of an in-stream and prints their contents. SetUpMeeting, "monitor calendar" daemons and "listener" daemons all send comments (by stuffing them in tuples and appending them to the in-stream) to the output process for printing. Thus, the output process prints comments that look like

```
*new meeting (id 3401) Tues 9 - 9:30 with 3*
```

or

```
*comment re 3401: "what for?" -- 3*
```

These output lines may wind up being interspersed with input lines; that's alright. (Those are the breaks when you're dealing with this kind of asynchronous system.)

Note that you'll have to make provision for initializing the system and creating each user's calendar in some starting state.

2. (*a*) Design and implement the following extensions to the meeting maker:

(*i*) *Best-effort scheduling.* If a requested meeting proves to be impossible to schedule, the system either looks for some other time not far from the requested interval during which it *can* be scheduled, or it schedules a meeting during the requested interval that omits some of (but not "too many" of) the specified attendees. It reports this best-effort result to the requestor, and asks whether the modified meeting should be ratified or cancelled.

(*ii*) *Calendar extension.* Toward the end of each month, the system automatically generates a next-month calendar tuple for each user, initialized to the same schedule (with regard to acceptable meeting hours) as the previous month's. The user must approve the new calendar tuple before it's installed. (Clearly, you now need a process that knows the current date.)

(*iii*) *Regular meetings with query.* The user may request that a certain meeting be scheduled not once but daily, weekly, monthly or whatever. After each occurrence of a regular meeting, the system asks the original scheduler whether the next meeting should in fact go ahead as planned.

(*iv*) *Priority meetings.* If a priority meeting is requested, the system attempts to override any existing appointments. First, it checks what conflicts will arise if the priority meeting is scheduled as planned. Next, it attempts to reschedule any preempted meetings, placing them as close as possible to their originally scheduled times. Then it reports the whole (tentative) arrangement to all parties to the priority meeting; if all agree, the meeting is scheduled; otherwise, the attempt fails.

(*v*) *Room scheduling.* Each user's calendar tuple notes how many people can be accommodated in his office. A "rooms tuple" holds a schedule for every public meeting room. When a meeting has been scheduled that is too big for the originator's office, the system picks a "convenient" public room, modifies the rooms tuple and reports the location as well as the time to all participants.

(*b*) Think up five more nice extensions. Implement them. (*c*) Is your system starting to sound like something that people might want to pay money for? What are you waiting for?

2. Chandy and Misra [CM88] present the following problem:

The problem is to find the earliest meeting time acceptable

to every member of a group of people. Time is integer valued
and nonnegative. To keep notation simple, assume that the
group consists of three people, F, G, and H. Associated
with persons F, G, and H are functions f, g, h (respectively),
which map times to times. The meaning of f is as follows
(and the meanings of g, h follow by analogy). For any t,
$f(t) \geq t$; person F can meet at time $f(t)$ and cannot meet at
any time u where $t \leq u < f(t)$. Thus $f(t)$ is the earliest time
at or after t at which person F can meet. [CM88, p. 12].

Chandy and Misra discuss several ways of solving the earliest meeting
time problem given functions f, g and h. In one approach, a proposed
meeting time (initially 0) is passed in a circuit from one participant
to the next; when F receives it, if the proposed time is t, F resets
the proposed time to $f(t)$ (and then hands the proposal on to G, who
does likewise, and so on). When the proposal makes a complete circuit
without changing, we're done. In another approach (somewhat modified
from a strategy [CM88] describes), each participant proposes a meeting
time; then each participant looks at the other proposals, and modifies
his own proposal accordingly; the cycle repeats until all proposals are
the same.

Implement both approaches. (A good strategy for the second involves
one single-source multi-sink read stream for each participant.)

3. Operating systems are sometimes structured as coordinated process ensembles. Write a simulated multi-process terminal input system
consisting of four concurrent processes plus a fifth for testing purposes.
The processes and their functions are

(a) `tty`: simulate a keyboard by generating a sequence of "input characters". The sequence is stored in tuple space as a stream. Characters can
be alphanumeric, or three special characters: BACKSPACE, LINEKILL
or NEWLINE. You can represent these characters in any way you want
(since your own program will be interpreting whatever character code
you use). To simulate a user's typing ok<RETURN>, your process generates

```
("tty", 1, <o>, ... )   /* you may need other fields */
("tty", 2, <k>, ... )
```

```
("tty", 3, <NEWLINE>, ... )
```

where `<char>` is your code for **char**. The **tty** process can generate arbitrary character streams for testing purposes.

We'll refer to the stream of characters generated by this process as the "tty stream". (Two processes, "echo" and "line-editor", will use the tty stream as input).

(*b*) **echo**: inspect each character in the tty stream. If it's an alphanumeric, print it. If it's a BACKSPACE, print a backspace. If it's a LINEKILL, print n backspaces, where n is the number of characters printed and not backspaced-over since the last NEWLINE. If it's a NEWLINE, print a newline.

(*c*) **line-editor**: inspect each character in the tty stream. If it's an alphanumeric, add it to the end of the current-line buffer. If it's a BACKSPACE, erase the most recently-added character; if it's a LINEKILL, erase all characters in the buffer. If it's a NEWLINE, remove the characters from the line buffer one-by-one and put them into an "edited" stream, which is structurally the same as the tty stream. For each new character added to the stream, increment a global "CharsAvail" counter, which will be stored in its own tuple.

(*d*) **supply-chars**: wait for get-character requests, attempt to meet the requests and return the results, by repeatedly executing the following outline:

```
in("get", ?id, wanted);
...
  out("got", id, char-string, count);
```

A client process that wants 5 characters will generate a

```
("get", id, 5)
```

request-tuple. **supply-chars** returns the requested number of characters by removing them from the "edited" stream, updating the **CharsAvail** tuple as appropriate; it returns the requested characters in a character string, together with a count of how many there are (*i.e.*, how long the string is). If the client asks for 5 and there are only 3 available, return all 3 together with a "count" of 3.

(e) The test-process should use a procedure (not a process) called
readchar. **readchar()** accepts as arguments a character count and
the address of a buffer; it deposits characters in the specified buffer, and
returns a character count. If I execute

```
count = readchar(5, &buff);
```

when three characters are available, the three characters are placed in
buff and 3 is returned. Assume that many different processes may
execute **readchar** concurrently (meaning that many different client processes all want to read input from the same stream).

☐ 4. (a) In chapter 3, you built a distributed data structure that realized
an abstract market. Beginning with the market structure, implement
a "stock ticker" process that prints out the price of each commodity
after each transaction. You can implement an "approximate ticker"
that uses a **changed** flag of the sort discussed above (why is such a
ticker "approximate"?), or you can implement an "exact ticker" that is
guaranteed to report each transaction. Test your system by creating a
collection of concurrent "trader" processes, each of which carries out a
series of transactions.

(b) Build a restricted version of your market: only a single commodity is
traded (the ticker, again, reports its current price). Create a collection
of trader processes. Each one repeatedly generates a random number
between 0 and 1. If the generated number is $< k_1$, the trader buys; if
it's $> k_2$, the trader sells ($0 \leq k_1 \leq k_2 \leq 1$). Store the values of k_1 and
k_2 in a tuple, where they can be changed as the program runs. Does
your market respond to relative increases in supply (sellers) and demand
(buyers) as it ought to?

(c) Build a new version of the market in which, as price rises, traders
display an increased propensity to sell and not to buy; as it falls, the
tendency to buy increases, and to sell decreases. Can you build a "self-
stabilizing system," in which heightened demand or supply creates only
a short-term change in prices?

(d) Finally, "customize" each trader. After each buy-or-sell decision,
traders look at the ticker. If the price has risen by more than U percent over the last t trades, or fallen by more than D percent over the
last t trades, a trader's behavior changes. In the former case he enters

speculate mode, in the latter case *panic* mode. In *speculate* mode, every rise in price *increases* a trader's propensity to buy. In *panic* mode, every *fall* in price increases a trader's tendency to *sell*. In "normal" mode, each trader's behavior is "self-stabilizing," as in part (*c*). The behavior thresholds *U* and *D* are *different* for each trader. If a "boom" is a consistent, self-sustaining rise in prices and a "panic" is a corresponding fall, can you build a system in which random price fluctuations can (occasionally) induce booms or panics?

☐ 5. The previous exercise centered on an "automatic" market—prices are determined by the number of buyers or sellers. Implement a system modelled on the meeting maker that supports a more realistic market, in which prices are set by negotiation among buyers and sellers. As in the original chapter 3 exercise, your system implements the routines buy() and sell(). Now, however, the first seller or buyer of some commodity creates a conversation stream (as discussed above); the stream exists for as long as there are outstanding requests to sell or buy that commodity. Executing buy(A, 100) causes the message "process Q offers $100" to be added to the relevant conversation stream. (Q's identity is supplied automatically by his "stockbroker" process.) sell works in a similar way. Traders must be able to add new offers and bids to an existing stream. The new system should have a stock ticker, as in the previous problem. (A more interesting ticker service would report volume as well as price.)

☐ (*Turingware:*) 6. Consider an "expert network" that represents a kind of generalization of the trellis architecture discussed in chapter 8. An expert has ≥ 1 *input streams* and a unique *output stream*. An expert is notified whenever a value appears on any one of its input streams. The expert may, in response, add a new value to its output stream (which may in turn cause other experts to be notified). (For example: if the weather expert attaches a snowstorm prediction to its output stream, or the mayor's office predicts a presidential visit, the highway department expert attaches a mobilization plan to its output stream, which may trigger, in turn, the costs-projection expert.) In many cases, these expert networks might be naturally trellis-shaped. But unlike trellises, they may have cycles (and hence, among other things, can't support realtime performance projections); and their data streams are explicitly *archival*. They may be *read* by any number of processes, but they are never *consumed*; they exist forever, creating a permanent record of the system's career.

Design and implement this kind of system for some arbitrary domain, in such a way that each expert can be *either* a process or a person. Persons should interface to the system in the same way processes do. Specifically: they should be notified (by a message printed on a terminal) whenever a new value is attached to one of their input streams; subsequently, they must be able to invoke (directly from a command interpreter) a routine that attaches some newly-computed value to their *own* output streams—whereupon other processes (or people) that depend on these output streams must be notified in turn.

(Note that, to read several streams, you'll need to create one stream-reader process for each. Each one of these processes reads a single stream, copying each newly-arriving element onto an input stream that is scanned directly by a decision process, or by a daemon representing a human decider. If this expedient distresses you, what simple extension to Linda would solve the problem?)

This sort of system, in which persons and processes come together in a single coordinated ensemble held together by distributed data structures, is a harbinger of the future, a fitting conclusion to the chapter and this book, and an introductory glance at a broad and fascinating new topic in computer science.

A C-Linda Reference Manual

A.1 Introduction

(This manual is derived from an earlier version by Donald Berndt.)

The reader is assumed to be familiar with the general character of tuples and tuple spaces, as described in chapter 3. In the following, the word *tuple* designates the argument to an `out` or `eval` operation; *anti-tuple* refers to the argument to an `in`, `inp`, `rd` or `rdp` operation. A tuple is a series of typed values, for example

```
("a string", 15.01, 17, x),
```

or

```
(0, 1).
```

An anti-tuple is a series of typed fields; some are values (or "actuals"), others are typed place-holders (or "formals"). A formal is prefixed with a question mark. For example,

```
("a string", ? f, ? i, y).
```

The first and last field are *actuals*; the middle two fields are *formals*.

A.2 C-Linda Operations

There are four basic C-Linda operations and two variant predicate forms. The operations `in()`, `inp()`, `rd()`, and `rdp()` remove information from tuples space; the out() and eval() generate tuples, with eval() implicitly handling process creation as well[1].

A.2.1   in()

The in() operation attempts to withdraw a specified tuple from tuple space. Tuple space is searched for a matching tuple against the anti-tuple supplied as the operation's argument. (Matching rules are discussed in the next section.) When and if a tuple is found, it is withdrawn from tuple space, and the values of its actual fields are bound to any corresponding formals in the anti-tuple. Tuples are withdrawn *atomically*: a tuple can be grabbed by only one process, and once grabbed it is withdrawn whole. If no matching tuple exists in tuple space, the process executing the in() suspends until a matching tuple becomes available. If many tuples satisfy the match criteria, one is chosen arbitrarily.

Examples. Assuming a tuple space full of coordinate pairs, we could write an in() to select any pair.

```
in("coord", ?x, ?y);
```

To match only those tuples with $x = 3$, we write a more specific in().

```
in("coord", 3, ?y);
```

A.2.2   rd()

The rd() operation is the same as in(), with actuals assigned to formals as before, *except* that the matched tuple remains in tuple space.

Example. Using the coordinate tuples again, we might augment them with an extra index field for organization as a distributed vector. Each

---

[1]The alternate operation names _linda_in, _linda_inp, _linda_rd, _linda_rdp, _linda_out, and _linda_eval are also provided. These names can be used if the shorter names conflict with other symbols.

tuple of the vector would look like ("coord vector", index, x, y). Processes can read this table by using rd:

```
for (i = 0; i < TABLE\_SIZE; ++i) {
  rd("coord table", i, ?x, ?y);
  ...
}
```

The above loop would read successive tuples from the "coord table".

A.2.3   inp() and rdp()

These operations attempt to locate a matching tuple and return 0 if they fail; otherwise, they return 1 and perform actual-to-formal assignment as described above. The only difference between the standard operations (in() and rd()) and the corresponding predicate forms is that the predicates will not block if no matching tuple is found.

A.2.4   out()

The tuple specified by an out() operation is evaluated and then added to tuple space. The executing process continues as soon as evaluation of the tuple is complete. (No specified action is taken in the event that tuple space is full. The current implementation will abort execution and print a diagnostic. Typically such events are treated by programmers along the lines of a stack or heap overflow in the context of conventional programming languages: the system is rebuilt with a larger tuple space. Future versions of the system may raise exception flags.)

Example. To create tuples for the first 100 integers and their square roots, we could use the following loop:

```
for (i = 0; i < 100; ++i)
  out("square roots", i, sqrt(i));
```

A.2.5   eval()

Executing an eval operation causes the following sequence of activities. First, bindings for names cited explicitly in the tuple are established in the environment of the eval-executing process. At this point, the eval-executing process may continue. Each field of the tuple argument to eval is now evaluated, independently of and asynchronously with the eval-executing process and each other. The fields of an eval tuple are evaluated *concurrently*: evaling a 5-field tuple implicitly creates 5 new threads of execution. When every field has been evaluated completely, the tuple consisting of the values yielded by each eval-tuple field, in the order of their appearance in the eval-tuple, becomes available in tuple space.

> *Limitations of the current implementation:* (1) Only expressions consisting of *a single function call* are evaluated within the "live tuple". All other expressions are evaluated *before new processes are created.* (2) Some current implementations in fact evaluate all fields of an eval tuple *sequentially* within a *single* new process. (In other words, they create only one new process per eval.)

Examples.

To create 100 parallel processes to perform some function on the first 100 integers, we could use a loop as follows:

```
for (i = 0; i < 100; ++i)
  eval("square roots", i, sqrt(i));
```

To create *n* worker processes, we could use

```
for (i = 0; i < n; ++i)
  eval("worker", worker());
```

A.3 Tuples and their matching rules

Tuple Field Types. The fields of a tuple have any of the following types:

1. [unsigned] int, long, short, and char

2. float and double

3. struct

4. union

5. [] (of arbitrary dimensions) of the above.

6. *, but only at the top level (as we discuss).

Fixed *vs.* **varying aggregates.** When it is used in a Linda operation, an aggregate (an array or a dynamically allocated chunk of memory) has an added attribute that is *not* part of its C declaration.

Arrays are often allocated for use as buffers which are intended to hold a varying number of elements over the course of a computation. In practice, such an array often has a *current length* that is different from (and sometimes much less than) its *allocated length*. If Linda failed to acknowledge this fact—if it insisted on treating arrays as fixed size objects only—large performance penalties could in some cases result. Linda accordingly assigns a *fixed/varying* attribute to each aggregate object that occurs in a tuple space operation. The length of a *fixed* aggregate is known (and fixed) at compile time. A *varying* aggregate uses additional information (provided at runtime) to specify its current length.

A ":" appearing after an aggregate name indicates that the named aggregate is *varying*; information about the current length follows the ":". A pointer always denotes a varying object, and must use the ":" notation. An array defaults to *fixed* (with the associated length being the declared size of the array), but can be made *varying* by the use of a ":".

To handle a common C idiom, these rules also apply to the **struct** type (see below).

Tuple Matching Rules.   Tuple matching entails a field-by-field comparison. Matching is defined as follows:

1. A tuple generated by **out** or **eval** matches an anti-tuple generated by **in** or **rd** exactly when the tuple and the anti-tuple have the same number of fields, and the ith field of the tuple matches the ith field of the anti-tuple.

2. A formal field and an actual field match exactly when their types and their sizes are the same.

    (a) The type of an aggregate field for matching purposes is its "base type." The base type of an array is the type of the array's elements. The base type of a pointer is the type of the object pointed to.

    (b) For **struct** or **union** fields, the type of the field is extended for matching purposes to include the structure or union name.

    (c) Scalar-type fields don't match aggregate-type fields. (For example, if p's type is **int** *, then *p and p:1 do *not* match).

    (d) Fixed aggregate-type fields match other fixed aggregate-type fields of the same length *only*. (Fixed aggregates do not match varying aggregates.)

3. Two actual fields match exactly when their types are the same and and their values are the same. Scalar actuals must have equal values[2].

    Aggregate actuals require agreement in number and value of elements.

Examples—scalar types. The following are all legal statements:

```
int i, *pi, pa[2], foo();
pi = &i;
```

---

[2]The programmer should be careful when using floating point values. The usual problems of inequality due to round-off and truncation can make matching unpredictable.

```
...
out("integer", i);
out("integer", 7);
out("integer", *pi); /* Note the '*'---this is not a
                        a varying aggregate. */
...
in("integer", ?i);
in("integer", ?i);
in("integer", ?*pi);
...
out("integer", pa[0]);
out("integer", foo());
...
in("integer", ?pa[0]);
in("integer", ?*(pa+1));
```

The following operations could all consume the tuple ("integer", 2):

```
i = 2;
...
in("integer", i);
in("integer", *pi);
in("integer", 2);
```

(Note that the statements out(&i) and out(pi) are *not* included among the examples above. A pointer to a scalar indicates an array or an aggregate, as described in the following sections.)

Examples—structure fields. The following statements illustrate the use of structure and pointer-to-structure fields. For structure-type fields to match, they must have the same size and the same structure tag. Structure values match only when they are identical on a byte-by-byte basis.

```
int len;
struct S s, *ps;
```

```
ps = &s;
...
out("structure", s);
out("structure", *ps);
...
in("structure", ?s);
in("structure", ?*ps);
...
```

Varying-length structure fields. The ":" notation may be used with
structures as well, in order to specify a structure size in *bytes*. In effect,
the structure is being treated as an array of bytes. This is designed to
accommodate the C idiom of a structure that has a varying length array
as its last element. Examples:

```
out("structure", s:);
out("structure", *ps:);
out("structure",
    s:sizeof(s)+(s.buf_len*sizeof(s.buf[0])));
...
in("structure", ?s:len);
in("structure", ?*ps:len);
```

Note this important difference:

```
out("structure", ps:i);  /* out i structures, which are
                            found beginning at ps. */
out("structure", *ps:i); /* out one structure,length i
                            bytes. */
```

Examples—*Fixed* Array Fields.

```
int a[20];
...
```

```
out("array", a);
...
in("array", ?a);
```

Examples—*Varying* **Array Fields** The general form of a varying array field is *array*: *length*: *limit* , where *array* is a pointer, *length* is the number of elements, and *limit* specifies a maximum number of elements. Thus, an entire array, or some portion of an array, can easily be added or removed from tuple space. In an out() operation, the length is used to determine how many elements should be added to tuple space. A constant, variable, or expression can be used to specify a length for an out(). The length of an actual array is also used for matching, indicating the amount of valid data for comparisons.

A formal varying array expects the length field to be a variable, and assigns to *length* the number of elements actually returned. The *limit* may can be used to supply a copy limit on the number of elements returned; its use is optional.

Limitation: limit fields are ignored in some current versions.

As an example, we out() an array using both explicit and implicit lengths:

```
int *pa, a[20], len, lim;

...
pa = a;
...
out("array", pa:20);
...
out("array", a:20);
...
out("array", a:);
```

The short-hand form out("array", a:), omitting a length, indicates a varying aggregate whose length is the declared length of the array. Note

that an explicit length *must* be used with pointers. When we in() the
whole array, the return value of len in both cases is 20:

```
in("array", ?pa:len);
...
in("array", ?a:len);
```

The first 10 elements of the above array can be specified in an out() as
follows:

```
out("array portion", pa:10);
...
out("array portion", a:10);
```

In order to retrieve one of the 10-element pieces created above, we could
write the following, which will result in len = 10.

> A data area used as a formal field must be big enough to
> hold the corresponding actual, or it must have an associated
> limit; otherwise, data may be corrupted.

```
in("array portion", ?pa:len);
...
in("array portion", ?pa:len:20);
```

The following examples use actuals on in() for matching both fixed and
varying arrays:

```
in("array", a);    /*fixed: must match all 20 elmnts */
in("array", a:20); /*varying: must match all 20 elmnts */
...
in("array", a:10); /*match chunk of exactly 10 elmnts */
```

Multidimensional Array Fields. Multidimensional arrays match only if the types of the referenced components are in agreement:

```
int a[3] [5] [2], b[4] [6] [2];
...
out("array component", a[0]);
in("array component", ?b[0]); /* match fails */
...
out("2-int component", a[0] [0]);
in("2-int component", ?b[0] [0]); /* match succeeds */
```

The first match fails since a "5x2-integer component" does not match a "6x2-integer component". The type of the array component being referenced in a particular operations is critical when matching. Using two similar arrays, a more thorough group of valid examples follows.

```
int a[3] [5] [2], c[3] [5] [2];

/* tuple generated by...*/
out("3x5x2-int fixed", a);
/* can be matched by...*/
in("3x5x2-int fixed", ?c);


/* tuple generated by...*/
out("3x5x2-int varying", a:);
/* can be matched by...*/
in("3x5x2-int varying", ?c:len);


/* tuple generated by...*/
out("3x5x2-int varying", a:3);
/* can be matched by...*/
in("3x5x2-int varying", ?c:len:3);
```

More matching pairs:

```
int d[5][2], e[2], i;

out("5x2-int fixed", a[0]);
in("5x2-int fixed", ?d);

out("5x2-int varying", a[0]:);
in("5x2-int varying", ?d:len);

out("5x2-int varying", a[0]:5);
in("5x2-int varying", ?d:len:5);



out("2-int fixed", a[0][0]);
in("2-int fixed", ?e);

out("2-int varying", a[0][0]:);
in("2-int varying", ?e:len);

out("2-int varying", a[0][0]:2);
in("2-int varying", ?e:len:2);

out("int", a[0][0][0]);
in("int", ?i);
```

String Fields. As in C, string fields are treated as arrays of type
char; the can be treated like any other kind of array. Note that in
C, the string constant "abcde" has type char [6] (C defines it with
a trailing null character). Except for this special case (since C doesn't
support any other array constants, no analogous usage exists for the
other scalar types), arrays of characters behave exactly like other arrays.
In particular, Linda operations are *not* sensitive to the null character.

The following statements are examples of character arrays in C-Linda
operations:

```
int len;
char s[10], *ps;
ps = s;

out("string", s);
in("string", ?s);

out("string", s:len);
in("string", ?s:len);

out("string", ps:len);
in("string", ?ps:len);
```

A 5-character string constant will only be matched by a 6 character array formal (the 6 characters being the 5 in the string plus the terminator):

```
char s[6];

out("string", "abcde");
in("string", ?s);
```

We can out() a varying character array using a short-hand ":" or an explicit length, forcing the terminator to be ignored. The corresponding in() can match either tuple; the returned length will be either 6 (if it matches the first tuple) or 5 (if it matches the second):

```
out("string", "abcde":);   /* size 6 */
out("string", "abcde":5);  /* size 5 */

in("string", ?s:len);
```

A.4   Invoking C-Linda

The C-Linda compiler is invoked via the "driver" program clc. clc
oversees a number of operations: a (1) C-Linda file (with extension
".cl") is parsed[3], its Linda operations are transformed into "normal"
C and data are collected about the operations, (2) the resulting C file is
compiled using the native C compiler (cc), and finally (3) the object file
and the descriptive information from the Linda operations are combined
to form a Linda object file (extension ".lo"). At link time, the ".lo"
files are analyzed as a whole, and the information yielded drives the
choice of efficient run-time support within the Linda kernel.

Multiple files (a mixture of object files, C source files and C-Linda source
files) may be specified. For example, the files foo.cl, bar.cl, baz.c
and biz.o can be compiled and linked using the command below; the
output will be the executable file a.out.

```
clc foo.cl bar.cl baz.c biz.o
```

The -o option may be used to give the output file some other name than
a.out. Since clc uses the native C compiler, other options provided by
cc may be supported.

The -c option allows individual C-Linda files to be compiled. The Linda
object files can then be linked at a later time:

```
clc -c foo.cl
clc -c bar.cl
clc -o foobar foo.lo bar.lo
```

Current versions require that the function real_main be
used as the top level routine in C-Linda programs (replacing
main).

A.4.1   clc options

The following options are interpreted by clc.

---

[3]Using a parser derived from the GNU C compiler.

-c Compile the specified files but do not link them. The object output
will be placed in "file.lo" if the source was a .cl file, "file.o" if
the source was a .c file.

-Dname or -Dname=def Define the symbol "name" for the preprocessor, as if a #define were part of the source. If no definition
(the "def" part above) is supplied, the value of the specified symbol defaults to 1.

-g The compiler and ld (via -lg) produce additional symbol table information for debugging.

-Idir Add the specified directory to the search path used for include
files.

-linda arg The ts <num> argument causes the program to be run with
a tuple space consisting of num 200-byte blocks. When tuple space
is exhausted, the message "out of tb's" appears. Once program
error has been ruled out as a possibility, increasing this size may
solve the problem. Tuple space size is reported in the initialization
message at runtime.

The tuple_scope argument causes the program to be compiled
with support for the X-based debugging tool TupleScope [Ber90].

-llib An ld flag: use "lib" for linking.

-Ldir Another ld flag: add "dir" to the library search path.

-o file Use "file" for clc output.

-O Use the C code improver.

-v List the subcommands (verbose mode) for each step in the compilation.

-w Suppress compiler warning messages. This does not suppress Linda
warning messages.

A.5   Timing and tracing tools

A.5.1   Timing Facilities

Three functions are provided within the C-Linda parallel programming environment for timing modules. The timing functions implement a stopwatch facility that is useful for collecting statistics on parallel execution and speedup factors.

The three timing functions are:

start_timer() Initializes and starts the stopwatch.

timer_split(*string*) Takes a time split (that is, a stopwatch reading) when called, and labels the time split with the specified string. The maximum string size is 32; the maximum number of timer splits is also 32.

print_times() Prints all time splits executed so far in tabular format with label strings.

A.5.2   Tracing Facilities

The C-Linda system provides for tuple tracing, allowing the programmer to monitor tuple traffic during the execution of a C-Linda parallel program. The C-Linda tracing facility is controlled by source code flags, the main C-Linda trace flag and a modifier flag for more detailed tracing.

LINDA_TRACE_ON Tracing is enabled and a trace message printed for each C-Linda operation executed. The basic message includes the process number, module name and line number. LINDA_TRACE_OFF disables tracing.

LINDA_ACTUALS_ON An additional trace message is printed, with the values of any actuals (e.g., fields for 0: 3.1415). LINDA_ACTUALS_OFF discontinues the additional trace message.

In order to use the tracing facilities, the file linda.h must be included using the standard C preprocessor #include command.

#include "linda.h"

The linda.h file contains all debugging flag definitions.

A.6 C-Linda Syntax

linda_call: call_type call_body

call_type: in | __linda_in |
inp | __linda_inp |
rd | __linda_rd |
rdp | __linda_rdp |
out | __linda_out |
eval | __linda_eval

call_body: (*element* { , *element* } *)

element: formal | actual

formal: ? *l-value [: length [: limit]] | type-name*

actual: r-value [: length]

length: expression

type-name: float | double | struct | union |
/unsigned/ (int | long | short | char)

The preface __linda_ is used to construct alternative operation names. These longer names can be used if the short names conflict with other symbols.

A.7   Quick Reference

Tuple input operations:

in(s) A tuple t that matches template s is withdrawn from TS; the
values of the actuals in t are assigned to the formals in s, and the
executing process continues. If no matching t is available when
in(s) executes, the executing process suspends until one is, then
proceeds as before. If many matching ts are available, one is chosen
arbitrarily.

rd(s) The same as in(s), with actuals assigned to formals as before,
except that the matched tuple remains in TS.

inp(s) **and** rdp(s) Predicate versions of in and rd, which attempt to
locate a matching tuple and return 0 if they fail; otherwise they
return 1, and perform actual-to-formal assignment as described
above.

Tuple output operations:

out(t) The tuple t is added to TS and the executing process continues
immediately.

eval(t) Similar to out(t), except that t is evaluated after rather than
before it enters tuple space; eval implicitly forks a new process to
perform the evaluation.

Programming rules:

- C-Linda files should end with a ".cl" extension.

- All C-Linda programs must have the top level function real_main
instead of main.

Bibliography

[ACD90]   V. Ambriola, P. Ciancarini, and M. Danelutto. Design and distributed implementation of the parallel logic language Shared Prolog. In *Proceedings Second ACM SIGPLAN Symposium on Principles and Practice of Parallel Programming*, pages 40–49, Seattle, March 1990.

[ACG89]   C. Ashcraft, N. Carriero, and D. Gelernter. Is explicit parallelism natural? Hybrid db search and sparse ldl^t factorization using Linda. Research report, Yale University Department of Computer Science, January 1989.

[ACGK88]   S. Ahuja, N. Carriero, D. Gelernter, and V. Krishnaswamy. Matching language and hardware for parallel computation in the Linda machine. *IEEE Transactions on Computers*, 37(8):921–929, August 1988.

[Ada82]   United States Department of Defense. *Reference Manual for the Ada Programming Language*, July 1982.

[AG89]   G. Almasi and A. Gottlieb. *Highly Parallel Computing*. Benjamin/Cummings, Redwood City, CA, 1989.

[AJ89]   R. Abarbanel and A. Janin. Distributed object management with Linda. Research report, Apple Computer, Cupertino, CA, September 1989.

[BA90]   M. Ben-Ari. *Principles of Concurrent and Distributed Programming*. Prentice-Hall, Hertfordshire, U.K., 1990.

[Bab84]   R. Babb. Parallel processing with large grain data flow techniques. *IEEE Computer*, 17:55–61, 1984.

[BCGL88]   R. Bjornson, N. Carriero, D. Gelernter, and J. Leichter. Linda, the portable parallel. Research Report 520, Yale University Department of Computer Science, January 1988.

[BDMN79]   G. Birtwistle, O. Dahl, B. Myhrhaug, and K. Nygaard. *Simula Begin*. Chartwell-Bratt, London, 1979.

[Ber90]   P. Bercovitz. TupleScope user's guide. Research report, Yale University Department of Computer Science, 1990.

[BHK88]   L. Borrman, M. Herdieckerhoff, and A. Klein. Tuple space integrated into Modula-2, implementation of the Linda concept on a hierarchical multiprocessor. In Jesshope and Reinartz, editors, *Proc. CONPAR '88*. Cambridge University Press, 1988.

[BN84]   A. Birrel and B. Nelson. Implementing remote procedure calls. *ACM Transactions on Computing Systems*, 2(1):39–59, February 1984.

[Bri75]   P. Brinch Hansen. The Programming Language Concurrent Pascal. *IEEE Transactions on Software Engineering*, 1(2):199–206, 1975.

[Bro90]   J. Browne. Software engineering of parallel programs in a computa-
            tionally oriented display environment. In D. Gelernter, A. Nicolau, and
            D. Padua, editors, *Languages and Compilers for Parallel Computing*,
            pages 75–94. MIT Press, Cambridge, 1990.

[BST89]   H. Bal, J. Stenier, and A. Tanenbaum. Programming Languages for
            Distributed Computing Systems. *ACM Computing Surveys*, 21(3):261–
            322, September 1989.

[BT87]   H. Bal and A. Tanenbaum. Orca: A language for distributed object-
            based programming. IR 140, Vrije Universiteit, Amsterdam, December
            1987.

[Car87]   N. Carriero. *Implementing Tuple Space Machines*. PhD thesis, Yale
            University Department of Computer Science, New Haven, Connecticut,
            1987. Department of Computer Science.

[CG89]   N. Carriero and D. Gelernter. Linda in context. *Communications of the
            ACM*, 32(4):444–458, April 1989.

[CG90]   N. Carriero and D. Gelernter. Tuple analysis and partial evaluation
            strategies in the Linda pre-compiler. In D. Gelernter, A. Nicolau, and
            D. Padua, editors, *Languages and Compilers for Parallel Computing*,
            pages 114–125. MIT Press, Cambridge, 1990.

[CGL86]   N. Carriero, D. Gelernter, and J. Leichter. Distributed data structures
            in Linda. In *Thirteenth ACM Symposium on Principles of Programming
            Languages Conf.*, pages 236–242, St. Petersburg, Florida, January 1986.
            Association for Computing Machinery.

[Che86]   M. C. Chen. A parallel language and its compilation to multiprocessor
            machines or VLSI. In *Thirteenth Annual ACM Symposium on Principles
            of Programming Languages*, pages 131–139. Association for Computing
            Machinery, January 1986.

[CM88]   K. M. Chandy and J. Misra. *Parallel Program Design: A Foundation*.
            Addison-Wesley, Reading, Mass., 1988.

[Com84]   D. Comer. *Operating System Design: The Xinu Approach*. Prentice-
            Hall, Englewood Cliffs, NJ, 1984.

[CZ85]   D. Cheriton and W. Zwaenpoel. Distributed process groups in the V
            Kernel. *ACM Transactions on Computer Systems*, 3(2):77–107, May
            1985.

[Dal88]   W. Dally. Object-oriented concurrent programming in CST. In *Proc.
            Third Conf. on Hypercube Concurrent Computers and Applications*,
            page 33, 1988.

[Dea69]   P. Deane. *The First Industrial Revolution*. Cambridge University Press,
            Cambridge, U.K., 1969.

[DSB88]   J. Dongarra, D. Sorenson, and P. Brewer. Tools and methodology for
            programming parallel processors. In M. Wright, editor, *Aspects of Com-
            putation on Asynchronous Processors*, pages 125 – 138. North-Holland,
            1988.

[Fac90]   M. Factor. *The Process Trellis Software Architecture for Parallel, Real-
            Time Monitors*. PhD thesis, Yale University Department of Computer
            Science, 1990. In preparation.

[FT89]   I. Foster and S. Taylor. *Strand: New Concepts in Parallel Programming*.
            Prentice-Hall, Englewood Cliffs, N.J., 1989.

[GCCC85]   D. Gelernter, N. Carriero, S. Chandran, and S. Chang. Parallel pro-
            gramming in Linda. In *International Conference on Parallel Processing*,
            pages 255–263, August 1985.

[Gil79]   P. Gilmore. Massive parallel processor (MPP): Phase one final report.
            Technical Report GER-16684, Goodyear Aerospace Co., Akron, 1979.

[GJ90]   D. Gelernter and S. Jagganathan. *Programming Linguistics: A first
            course in the design and evolution of programming languages*. MIT
            Press, Cambridge, 1990.

[GJL87]   D. Gelernter, S. Jagannathan, and T. London. Environments as first-
            class objects. In *Fourteenth ACM Symposium on Principle of Program-
            ming Languages Conf.*, January 1987.

[GR87]   L. Greengard and V. Rokhlin. A fast algorithm for particle simulations.
            Journal of Computaional Physics, 73:325–348, 1987.

[Hal85]   R. Halstead. Multilisp: A language for concurrent symbolic computa-
            tion. *Transactions on Programming Languages and Systems*, 7(4):501–
            538, October 1985.

[Hen82]   P. Henderson. Purely functional operating systems. In J. Darlington,
            P. Henderson, and D. Turner, editors, *Functional Programming and its
            Applications*, pages 177–192. Cambridge University Press, 1982.

[HH80]   P. Horowitz and W. Hill. *The Art of Electronics*. Cambridge Press,
            1980.

[Hoa74]   C. A. R. Hoare. Monitors: An operating system structuring concept.
            Communications of the ACM, 17(10):549–557, October 1974.

[Hoa78]   C. A. R. Hoare. Communicating sequential processes. *Communications
            of the ACM*, 21(8):667–677, August 1978.

[HS86]   W. D. Hillis and G. Steele Jr. Data parallel algorithms. *Communications
            of the ACM*, 29(12):1170–1183, December 1986.

[JLHB88]   E. Jul, H. Levy, N. Hutchinson, and A. Black. Fine-grained mobil-
            ity in the emerald system. *ACM Transactions on Computer Systems*,
            6(1):109–133, Feb. 1988.

[Jor86]   H. Jordan. Structuring parallel algorithms in an MIMD, shared memory environment. *Parallel Computing*, 3:93–110, 1986.

[Kah74]   G. Kahn. The semantics of a simple language for parallel processing. In *Proceedings IFIP Congress*, page 471, 1974.

[Kal89]   L. Kale. The design philosophy of the Chare kernel parallel programming system. Technical Report UIUCDCS-R-89-1555, University of Illinois at Urbana-Champaign Department of Computer Science, 1989.

[KL79]   H. Kung and C. Leiserson. Systolic arrays (for VLSI). In I. Duff and G. Stewart, editors, *Sparse Matrix Proceedings 1978*, pages 256–282. SIAM, 1979.

[Lel90]   W. Leler. Linda meets Unix. *IEEE Computer*, 23(2):43–55, Feb. 1990.

[LR80]   B. Lampson and D. Redell. Experience with processes and monitors in Mesa. *Communications of the ACM*, 23(2):105–117, Feb. 1980.

[LSF88]   C. Lee, S. Skedzielewski, and J. Feo. On the implementation of applicative languages on shared-memory, MIMD multiprocessors. In *Proceedings of the ACM/SIGPLAN Symposium on Parallel Programming*, Aug. 1988.

[Mal88]   T. Malone. What is coordination theory? Working Paper 182, MIT Center for Information Systems Research, Feb. 1988.

[May83]   D. May. OCCAM. *ACM SIPLAN Notices*, 18(4):69 – 79, April 1983.

[MC82]   T. Marsland and M. Campbell. Parallel search of strongly ordered game trees. *ACM Computing Surveys*, 14(4):533–552, Dec. 1982.

[MK88]   S. Matsuoka and S. Kawai. Using tuple space communication in distributed object-oriented languages. In *Proceedings OOPSLA '88*, pages 276–284, Nov. 1988.

[MT86]   S. Mullender and A. Tanenbaum. The design of a capability-based distributed operating system. *The Computer Journal*, 29(4):289–300, Mar. 1986.

[Nar88]   J. Narem. Db: A parallel news database in Linda. Techincal memo, Yale University Department of Computer Science, Aug. 1988.

[NPA86]   R. Nikhil, K. Pingali, and Arvind. Id Nouveau. Memo 265, MIT Computation Structures Group, 1986.

[Ols86]   T. Olson. Finding lines with the Hough Transform on the BBN Butterfly parallel processor. Report 10, University of Rochester, Department of Computer Science, Butterfly Project, Sept. 1986.

[Rin88]   G. Ringwood. Parlog86 and the dining logicians. *Communications of the ACM*, 31(1):10–25, Jan. 1988.

[Sei85]   C. Seitz. The Cosmic Cube. *Communications of the ACM*, 28(1):22–33, 1985.

[Sha87]   E. Shapiro, editor. *Concurrent Prolog Collected Papers*, volume 1 and 2. MIT Press, Cambridge, Mass., 1987.

[Sny90]   L. Snyder. The XYZ abstraction levels of poker-like languages. In D. Gelernter, A. Nicolau, and D. Padua, editors, *Languages and Compilers for Parallel Computing*, pages 470–489. MIT Press, Cambridge, 1990.

[Tan87]   A. Tanenbaum. *Operating Systems: Design and Implementation*. Prentice-Hall, Englewood Cliffs, N.J., 1987.

[WH90]   S. Ward and R. Halstead. *Computation Structures*. MIT Press, Cambridge, 1990.

[Wie48]   N. Wiener. *Cybernetics*. John Wiley and Sons, New York, 1948.

[Wir77]   N. Wirth. Modula: A language for modular multiprogramming. *Software—Practice and Experience*, 7:3–35, 1977.

[WL88]   R. Whiteside and J. Leichter. Using Linda for supercomputing on a local area network. In *Proceedings of Supercomputing 88*, 1988.

[You87]   M. Young. The duality of memory and communication in the implementation of a multiprocessor operating system. In *Proceedings of the Eleventh ACM Symposium on Operating Systems Principles*, pages 63–76, Nov. 1987.

Index

The MIT Press, with Peter Denning as general consulting editor, publishes computer science books in the following series:

ACM Doctoral Dissertation and Distinguished Dissertation Awards

Artificial Intelligence
Patrick Winston, founding editor
Michael Brady, Daniel Bobrow, and Randall Davis, editors

Charles Babbage Institute Reprint Series for the History of Computing
Martin Campbell-Kelly, editor

Computer Systems
Herb Schwetman, editor

The MIT Electrical Engineering and Computer Science Series

Exploring with Logo
E. Paul Goldenberg, editor

Foundations of Computing
Michael Garey and Albert Meyer, editors

History of Computing
I. Bernard Cohen and William Aspray, editors

Information Systems
Michael Lesk, editor

Logic Programming
Ehud Shapiro, editor; Koichi Furukawa, Jean-Louis Lassez, Fernando Pereira, and David H. D. Warren, associate editors

Research Monographs in Parallel and Distributed Processing
Christopher Jesshope and David Klappholz, editors

Scientific and Engineering Computation
Janusz Kowalik, editor

Technical Communications
Ed Barrett, editor